The Gospel of Genesis

Studies in Protology and Eschatology

The Gospel of Genesis

Studies in Protology and Eschatology

by

Warren Austin Gage

Wipf and Stock Publishers
150 West Broadway • Eugene OR 97401
2001

The Gospel of Genesis
Studies in Protology and Eschatology
By Gage, Warren Austin
Copyright©1984 by Gage, Warren Austin
ISBN: 1-57910-608-0

Reprinted by *Wipf and Stock Publishers*
150 West Broadway • Eugene OR 97401

Previously published by Carpenter Books, 1984.

for Bruce K. Waltke

Table of Contents

Part I. The Gospel of Genesis

Part II. A Meditation on Genesis 1–12

Foreword

Robert Alter in his superb book, *The Art of Biblical Narrative* (1981)—a work marred, however, by his view that biblical narrative is prose fiction—equips us for Warren Gage's remarkably penetrating insights into the relation of Genesis 1-7 to the rest of the Bible. Alter noted that repetitive devices found in biblical narrative compare favorably with techniques or repetition found in the whole spectrum of narration from Homer to Günter Grass:

> Certain characteristic biblical uses of repetition closely resemble the kinds of repetition that are familiar artistic devices in short stories and novels, dramatic and epic poems, written elsewhere and later (p. 91).

He illustrated his view from the story of the Gentile prophet, Balaam, an illustration upon which I will elaborate (see Numbers 22-24). Within this story there is an episode involving Balaam and his donkey (Num 22:21-34) which foreshadows the relationship of Balak, king of Moab, and Balaam (Numbers 23-24). In a nutshell, what the donkey is to Balaam, the prophet is to the king. There are at least seven correspondences uniting these two episodes.

First, as Balaam rides his donkey to put his hex on Israel as Balak had requested, the donkey sees the angel of the LORD standing in the road with a drawn sword in his hand, but the prophet cannot see him. In the same way, after Balaam met Balak at their rendevouz, Balaam notes in his first prophecy: "From the rocky peaks I see them, from the heights I view them. I see a people . . ." (Num 23:9) and he prefaces his last two prophecies: "The oracle of Balaam son of Beor, the oracle of one whose eye

ix

sees clearly" (24:3), to which he adds in the last one, "who sees a vision of the Almighty, who falls prostrate, and whose eyes are opened" (24:16). But Balak is blind to the heavenly vision.

Second, the donkey sees the angel on three successive occasions (22:23, 25, 27) and blurts out finally, "You beat me these three times" (v 28), just as after Balaam saw God's blessing on Israel three times Balak exclaims, "I summoned you to curse my enemies, but you have blessed them these three times" (24:10).

Third, the donkey becomes progressively stubborn, and as Alter noted, "each time with a more discomfiting effect on her rider: first he is carried into the field, then he is squeezed against a fence, and finally the ass simply lies down under him." So also Balaam's blessings on Israel become progressively greater: first, the people are spread out like "the dust in number," second, they crouch "like a lion that does not rest till he devours his prey and drinks the blood of his victims"; and then, they spread out "like valleys, like gardens beside a river, like aloes planted by the LORD, like cedars beside the waters." In the fourth and markedly climactic vision Israel's king rises "like a star."

Fourth, the luckless rider who set out to destroy a nation becomes increasingly furious when his donkey does not respond to his proddings and beatings. At length he exclaims, "You have made a fool of me! If I had a sword in my hand, I would kill you right now." Likewise Balaam's prophecies finally make Balak's anger flare out against the prophet. Striking his hands together in a rage, he says, "Now leave at once and go home!" It is instructive to note in this connection that Balaam cannot kill the donkey and Balak cannot kill the prophet.

Fifth, the donkey speaks when "the LORD opened the donkey's mouth," and Balaam can speak only what the LORD put in his mouth when the Spirit of God comes upon him (23:3, 12, 16, 26, 24:2, 12–13).

Sixth, the ass has heretofore served Balaam well (Num 22:30), which must have been Balaam's habitual behavior with Balak; otherwise he would not have persistently summoned him.

Seventh, Balak does not notice the miracle that his donkey is talking. Alter commented, "He responds as though he were accustomed to having daily domestic wrangles with his asses" (Num 22:29). Just as amazingly, Balak remains unmoved by the miracle of divine prophecy.

With this illustration in hand we can now turn to Alter's analysis of repetitive techniques found across the board in narratives.

(1) *Key words* bind narratives together: e.g., in the Balaam story "see," "words in mouth," "blessing" and "curses," etc.

(2) *Motifs*, that is, as Alter defined them, "concrete images, sensory qualities, actions or objects that recur through a particular narrative," also weave the two episodes together into a unified whole. For example, "morning" (22:21 and 22:41), the servants with Balaam (22:22), and the princes with Balak (22:40).

(3) *Theme*, which according to Alter is "an idea which is part of the value-system of the narrative—it may be moral, moral-psychological, legal, political, historiosophical, theological—is made evident in some recurring pattern." The themes of revelation and inspiration run through the two episodes constituting the Balaam story.

(4) *Sequence of actions*, of which Alter said, "This pattern appears most commonly and clearly in folktale form of three consecutive repetitions, or three plus one, with some intensification or increment from one occurrence to the next, usually concluding either in a climax or a reversal. (For example, . . . Balaam's failure to direct the ass three times.)"

We may well pause here and ask about the value of these techniques. At least four reasons suggest themselves:

(1) Such foreshadowings involving these repetitive devices function as unifying devices producing a beautiful interwoven wholeness. In the case under consideration Balaam's journey to Moab on the back of his donkey becomes an integral part of the whole story.

(2) Repetition provides a focus on key ideas and promotes the development and intensification of the story to its climax.

(3) These repetitions also establish a kind of rhythm that clearly suggests events in history occur according to a preordained pattern. Whereas pagan man felt himself indissolubly connected with the Cosmos and the cosmic rhythms, the covenant community feels itself connected with history and the rhythms of history, as suggested by Mircea Eliade in *The Myth of the Eternal Return* (1954, p. xiiif.).

(4) These foreshadowings are enigmatic, that is, they serve both to conceal and reveal—to reveal to the astute and the discerning reader and to conceal from the obtuse and dull.

Gage proves himself to be a perspicacious student of Scripture; he opens up for the sensitive reader insights into the vast panorama of God's creative and redemptive work. Through his observations on the repetition of the foreshadowings found in Genesis 1–7 in the rest of Scripture one perceives with new conviction the fingerprint of God in history and his signature in the Bible. Just as the first episode in the Balaam narrative serves as a foreshadowing of the main story, so also the Old Testament serves as a foreshadowing of the New, and the two together constitute a beautifully interwoven whole. But even more particularly, Genesis 1–7 proves to be integrated with the rest of Genesis and Genesis with the rest of the Old Testament and the Old with the New.

Not all the author's correspondences will carry equal conviction with Gage's audience, but most will. Those that carry the most conviction are those that fit the above kinds of repetitions suggested by Alter. Throughout the work one will note Gage's appeal to "key-word" (e.g., "rule" [Gen 1:28; Num 24:19; etc.]), "motifs" (e.g., "ten" words in Genesis 1 and Exodus 20 [= Deuteronomy 5]); "themes" (e.g., the five themes that constitute the heart of the study); and "sequence of actions" (e.g., "microcosmic reenactments of creation").

BRUCE K. WALTKE

Preface

It is a delight to an author to remember those who helped him conceive and conclude his work. The thesis paper entitled "Eschatological Structure of Genesis" was first read at a colloquium presided over by Prof. Dr. Otto Betz during the Winter Semester 1979–80 in Tübingen. His kind encouragement was most helpful. A special note of gratitude is offered to Dr. Gregory K. Beale for his germinal ideas on irony represented in the "Oracle of Destiny" paper, along with his kind criticism and constant friendship during the years of study and preparation. The greatest debt of the author is expressed to Kenneth C. Olles, beloved co-pastor and special friend, for his vision of the "City of God," and for his encouraging our church upon that happy homeward pilgrimage to the heavenly Zion. The work likewise represents the contribution of Dr. Ferris L. McDaniel, who typed the manuscript and offered encouragement and criticism, and my beloved wife Betty, who proofread the manuscript.

This thesis was not conceived under the shade of academic bowers, nor was it prepared in the still obscurity of the pastor's study, but amid the distraction and disquietude of the local church, amidst the heartaches and joys of the people of God, the "little flock" in Covenant Community Church. The papers are brief, to spare the pastor the responsibility of redeeming his time. The commentary was prepared for the assembly, under the conviction that Genesis is as much a Gospel as John, that Moses is as much an evangelist as Matthew. May this little volume be used to the honor of the Lord Jesus, who first spoke peace to the heart of the author, making him to know the joy of forgiveness and the happiness of hope.

WARREN AUSTIN GAGE
University Park, Texas

The Gospel of Genesis

1 | Introduction

The Subject

The relationship of the biblical beginning and ending is a study of such sweeping scope and presuppositional import that it affects virtually any scriptural subject. Questions regarding the unity of the Bible, the relationship of the Old Testament to the New Testament, the hermeneutic of typology, and the relationship of biblical to systematic theology are but a few of the most current theological issues decisively affected by such a study. Nevertheless, since the publication in 1895 of Hermann Gunkel's pioneering classic *Schöpfung und Chaos in Urzeit und Endzeit*,[1] there has been a noticeable lack of scholarly investigation into so promising a subject. This work represents an attempt to discover the nature of the relationship between the biblical protology and eschatology.

The Possibility of the Study

It should be stated at the outset that such a study requires a unity of divine revelatory purpose transcending the testaments on the one hand, and a consistency of canonical (prophetic and apostolic) interpretation of that purpose on the other.[2]

Both testaments witness to God's overarching self-revelation. To Isaiah God declares the end from the beginning (46:9–10), while to John God is the Alpha and Omega, the First and the Last, the Beginning and the End (Rev 22:13). The unity of God's historical purpose is furthermore of such a knowable character that Christ would excoriate the religious leaders who could see

[1] H. Gunkel, *Schöpfung und Chaos in Urzeit und Endzeit* (Göttingen: Vandenhoeck & Ruprecht, 1895).
[2] These presuppositions are generally denied by higher criticism, suggesting, perhaps, the reason for the lack of scholarly investigation into protology and eschatology.

such consistency in nature (regarding a matter as capricious as the weather), but would not see similar consistency in grace (that is, that Jerusalem had become like unrepentant Nineveh, cf. Matt 16:1–4).

From beginning to end the biblical authors present a consistent, albeit selective (therefore interpretive) history.[3] For example, to Moses the exodus deliverance is the decisive theme of Pentateuchal history[4] to which the story of creation, the record of the flood, the narrative of Abraham's sojourn in Egypt and the Joseph stories are logically subordinate.[5] Likewise, the prophets so interpreted the captivity of Israel as requiring God to accomplish a second exodus for his people (cf. Isa 51:9–11; Jer 23:7–8). Similarly the apostles interpreted the Christ-event as the deliverance of God's Son from Egypt (Matt 2:15), the slaying of the passover Lamb (1 Cor 5:7), and the accomplishment of a greater exodus (Luke 9:31, Greek text) resulting in the deliverance of God's people from the sea (Rev 15:1–8). It is this capacity of the biblical authors to interpret history, expressing a commonality of theme due to a consistency in the divine governance of history, that makes possible a comprehensive study of protology and eschatology.[6]

The Method of the Study

The thesis of this study is that Genesis 1–7 constitutes a paradigm for macrocosmic (world) and microcosmic (Israelite) history; that is, that the history of the prediluvian temple-cosmos is synthetically paralleled in the histories of the postdiluvian

---

[3] Cf. the cyclical historiography of the author of Judg 2:11–23. Cf. further the moral historiography of the Chronicler.

[4] That is, Moses will introduce Yahweh as Elohim, not Elohim as Yahweh.

[5] The creation is elaborately reenacted in the exodus-eisodus redemption from Egypt. Noah, like Moses, is delivered by the ark from the waters. These themes will be considered in some detail later. The Abrahamic sojourn in Egypt (Gen 12:10–20) unfolds with (1) a famine to move Abraham to Egypt, (2) the jeopardy of the promised seed, (3) the plagues upon the house of pharaoh, and (4) the driving out of Abraham with much treasure—i.e., the story of the exodus in brief. Joseph, like Moses, is rejected by Israel only to be appointed by God for his deliverance (cf. Acts 7:9, 25).

[6] The unity of the Bible, in spite of the length of the inscripturational process and the diversity of authorship, evidences its inspiration. Who, for example, would attempt to synthesize major medical writings from Galen to the present?

temple-cosmos, the first Temple of Israel (from exodus to exile) and the second Temple of Israel (from second exodus to second exile).

The method of this study will be first to distinguish structural parallels in these historical records (reflecting a consistency of divine purpose in these events),[7] and second, to validate these parallels literarily (demonstrating concord with the prophetic interpretation of these events). The thesis chapter entitled "The Eschatological Structure of Genesis" distinguishes five themes consistently paralleled throughout macrocosmic history: the doctrines of God, Man, Sin, Redemption, and Judgment.[8] Each of these major themes derived from Genesis 1–7 is then traced through the scripture. First, God is considered as the protological Creator and the eschatological Redeemer. Second, Adam as the first man is compared with Christ as the last Man. Third, the protological fall of man into cursing is considered in view of the prophecy of the eschatological restitution of man to blessing. Fourth, the earthly Edenic beginning is compared with the promise of Edenic Zion in the end. Fifth, the protological pattern of the Noahic judgment is considered with regard to its eschatological recurrence.[9]

The Hope

It is the hope of the author that these studies might encourage the faithful regarding the trustworthiness of God's Word, while convicting the critic who would gainsay the scripture. May all who read be encouraged to acknowledge Christ crucified as the very Wisdom of God, surpassing the wisdom of man.

[7] The procedure here is to identify historical parallelism in prophetic prose, much as we identify conceptual parallelism in poetry. This principle of parallelism expresses itself historically, for example, in the recurrence of ritual reenactment (Passover, the Lord's Supper), redemptive recapitulation (the Christian's life reproduces his Lord's, Rom 6:8; 8:17; Gal 2:20), and in typological interpretation (cf. Christ as the new Adam, Moses, David, Solomon, and Jonah).

[8] The significance of these themes is suggested by their recapitulation. These categories, moreover, suggest a bridge from biblical to systematic theology. Cf. the doctrines of theology proper, anthropology, hamartiology, ecclesiology, and eschatology.

[9] These five models, along with their constituent parts, are displayed in the chart appended to chapter 2.

2 | The Eschatological Structure of Genesis

In a fascinating paragraph from his classic work, *Schöpfung und Chaos in Urzeit und Endzeit*,[1] Hermann Gunkel observed the fundamental interdependence between the beginning and ending of biblical history. He noted implicit reference to this relationship in 2 Pet 3:6–7 (where eschatological judgment is described after the dimensions of the Noahic catastrophe), and explicit formulation of it both in Matt 24:37, "But as the days of Noah were, so shall also the coming of the Son of Man be;" and Barnabas 6:13, "Behold, I make the end like the beginning."[2] Gunkel admitted his inability to discover the nature of the relationship between the biblical beginning and ending, though he postulated major theological significance to this relationship, stating his view that the New Testament speculation regarding predestination was in large part founded upon the comparison of first and last things.[3]

Claus Westermann marvelled in *Anfang und Ende in der Bibel*[4] that Gunkel could leave a question of such significance unresolved, for its answer is fundamental to the very thesis of his book. Westermann noted further that Gunkel's question has not yet been satisfactorily answered, though he likewise concluded that it remains of utmost theological import.

Gunkel's failure to investigate further the interrelationship of the biblical beginning and ending is consistent with a broader neglect of foundational studies in biblical protology, an omission which has hindered the successful construction of an eschatological scheme comprehending the entire scope of scripture. It

---

[1] H. Gunkel, *Schöpfung und Chaos*, p. 369.
[2] Matt 24:37: ὥσπερ γὰρ αἱ ἡμέραι τοῦ Ηῶε, οὕτως ἔσται ἡ παρουσία τοῦ υἱοῦ τοῦ ἀνθρώπου.; *Barn.* 6:13: ἰδού ποιῶ τὰ ἔσχατα ὡς τὰ πρῶτα.
[3] Gunkel, *Schöpfung und Chaos*, p. 369.
[4] C. Westermann, *Anfang und Ende in der Bibel* (Stuttgart: Calwer, 1969), p. 30.

seems only reasonable, however, that any accurate formulation of biblical eschatology should be squarely based upon biblical protology, that the ending of history could only be comprehensible within the categories by which the beginning of history is described. Furthermore, should Genesis provide us with an overarching structure of historical direction we might reasonably expect to discern the interrelationship of the biblical beginning and ending, and in so doing derive the theological insight which, though anticipated by Gunkel, nevertheless eluded him.

At first glance perhaps it appears paradoxical to suggest a telic or futurist theology undergirding Genesis, the book of origins and first things. Nevertheless the possibility of deriving an eschatological structure from Genesis follows from the fact that a comprehension of universal time is clearly within the self-consciousness of the book. This awareness of diachronology is suggested by the introductory "in the beginning" (בְּרֵשִׁית) of Gen 1:1, an expression which sets forth the beginning of history while implying a historical eventuation in an eschatological "ending of days" (אַחֲרִית הַיָּמִים),[5] and required by the promise of perpetual seasons in Gen 8:22, "While the earth remains (עֹד כָּל־ יְמֵי הָאָרֶץ), a statement wherein the prophetic oracle foresees an eschatological terminus.[6] Moreover, the possibility of projecting such an eschatological structure beyond Genesis is suggested by the divine teleology presupposed in the creation narrative[7] and consistently reaffirmed throughout scripture.[8] Genesis is, after all, the beginning of the revelation of the One who writes history from the Alpha to the Omega, who is the First and the Last, the Beginning and the End (Rev 22:13).

While the chronicle of the origin of Israel is unquestionably primary to the design of Genesis, the beginnings of Israel's national history are nevertheless embedded in a matrix of universal history, a broader context which affords a historiographical perspective to the author's interpretation of Israel's destiny.[9] This

---

[5] W. Eichrodt, *Theologie des Alten Testaments*, 2 vols. (Leipzig: J. C. Hinrichs, 1935) vol. 2, pp. 2–3, 53.

[6] Westermann, *Schöpfung* (Stuttgart: Kreuz-Verlag, 1971), p. 37.

[7] Cf. Gen 1:31.

[8] Cf. the worship formulation of Rev 4:11. The reasoning regarding teleology is often associated with the Genesis cosmology, e.g., Ps 104:31; Isa 43:18; John 1:13.

[9] Mosaic authorship of Genesis is implied by Christ in John 7:21-22.

introductory chronicle of universal history (Genesis 1–11), however, is constructed about a scheme by which the direction of the whole of history may be deduced and displayed.

The thesis of this chapter is that the chronicle of prediluvian history (Genesis 1–7) is composed of five theologically fundamental narratives, each of which finds consecutive, synthetic parallel in the history (and prophecy) of the postdiluvian world. Consequently, by understanding the historical movement initiated in early Genesis, we may discern the relationship between the beginning and ending of biblical history.

The first of these theological narratives is the original creation of the world out of the waters of chaos, a story foundational to theology proper and paralleled in postdiluvian history in the recreation of the world out of the waters of Noah. The second narrative is the commissioning of Adam, a record fundamental to anthropology, and paralleled in the new commission to Noah. The third narrative is the sin of Adam, a record finding hamartiological parallel in the sin of Noah. The fourth parallel concerns the relationship between the descendants of Adam, namely, the Cainites of the wicked city of Enoch and the Yahweh worshipers in the family of Seth. This chronicle of redemptive import finds parallel in the postdiluvian juxtaposition of the descendants of Noah, namely, the inhabitants of the wicked city of Babel and the Yahweh worshipers in the family of Abraham. Finally, the fifth parallel narrative concerns the sons of God and the daughters of man whose miscegenation brings universal judgment upon the ancient world. This record has profound eschatological significance as it projects the expectations of apostasy and cosmic catastrophe upon the biblical understanding of postdiluvian history.[10] The task of this study is to demonstrate that the record of postdiluvian history is stylized so as to be essentially a reduplicative chronicle of antediluvian history.[11] Accordingly, the five narrative models isolated and identified in the thesis statement will be

---

[10] Cf. Deut 31:14–32:43; Matt 24:37; 2 Pet 3:6–7.

[11] The notion of Semitic parallelism as a literary form is a well-accepted point of Hebrew exegesis. The interrelationship of the creative Word and history in Hebrew theological thought is also generally acknowledged. If the creative Word, then, and history are so inextricably identified in ancient oriental thought, might we not be justified in distinguishing a parallelism of history in Hebrew prose much as we distinguish a parallelism of thought in Hebrew poetry? The scope of this question is relevant to the hermeneutic of Old Testament history as

examined in turn and appeal will be made to the consecutive
structural and literary correspondence of the postdiluvian to the
prediluvian models. The literary correspondences marshalled to
defend the thesis are structurally presented, for it is to be observed
that the five parallel narratives sustain a logical as well as a
chronological consecution (i.e., God, man, sin, redemption, and
judgment).

It should be recognized that the primary goal of this survey is
to articulate the thesis directively and not exhaustively. It is freely
acknowledged that individual correspondences may be challenged
while other parallels may be suggested. Nevertheless it is hoped
that the aggregate of the evidence herein presented is sufficient to
sustain the broader profile of the thesis.

Genesis 8: The New Creation

The ordering of the present heavens and earth out of the
chaotic overthrow of the ancient world recorded in Genesis 8
parallels the original creation account of Genesis 1.[12] In both
chapters the theological narrative moves from the display of
divine work to the account of divine rest. In Genesis 8:1 God
brings about a wind to pass over the waters of the flood which,
like the waters of original chaos (Gen 1:2), cover the earth (Gen
7:18-19). The emergence of the dry land and the bringing forth of
vegetation (Gen 1:12) find a mirror image in the olive leaf brought
to Noah, which is taken as a token of the emergence of dry land
(Gen 8:11). Noah's sabbatical pattern in the sending of the dove[13]
suggests that God alone, who created the first world in six days,
can deliver the earth from such a catastrophe. The sabbath rest of

---

well as the understanding of New Testament typology; cf. the charts appended to
this chapter and to chapter 7.

[12] Compare the synthesis of original creation and the Noahic recreation in
the theology of the wisdom school in Pss 104:9; 74:12-17; Job 38:4-11; cf. also
2 Pet 3:5-7.

[13] The origin of the dove as a symbol of the Spirit (cf. Matt 3:16) may be
traceable to a synthesis of these creation accounts. Gen 1:2 describes the original
earth in darkness and deep (both to be taken as tokens of evil as indicated by their
absence in the perfected heavens and earth vision of Rev 21:1, 25), the Spirit of
God hovering upon the face of the waters (cf. the רָחַף of the eagle in Deut 32:11).
Noah sends forth first the raven (black and unclean) and then the dove (white and
clean), the dove finding no rest upon the waters of wickedness, therefore "hovering" upon them.

God at the conclusion of the original creation ("and He rested," וַיִּשְׁבֹּת, Gen 2:2) finds correspondence in the sacrificial rest of God after the new creation is completed ("and the Lord smelled the aroma of rest," רֵיחַ הַנִּיחֹחַ; Gen 8:21; cf. Exod 20:11 in which the rest of God on the seventh day of creation is described by the verb נוּחַ). The literary correspondence between both accounts is readily evident through the extent and frequency of shared vocabulary: שָׁבַת, לְמִינֵהוּ, יַבָּשָׁה/יָבֵשׁ, לַיְלָה/יוֹם, תְּהוֹם, רוּחַ.[14]

Genesis 9: The New Adam

The divine commission and blessing bestowed upon Noah finds precise parallel in the record of Adam.[15] The anthropologically fundamental doctrine of the divine image in man (צֶלֶם) occurs in the Adam narrative as the basis of man's identity and in the Noah narrative as the basis of man's protection, being wholly unique in Genesis to the Adam and Noah stories (Gen 1:27; 5:1, 3; 9:6). Surely it also has anthropological significance that man in his relationship to other animate life is a point central to both the Adam and Noah records.[16] God brings the נֶפֶשׁ-animals to Adam to be named. He brings them once again to Noah to be protected (cf. Gen 2:19 and 7:15).[17] Finally, the blessing of fruitfulness given to Adam and again to Noah virtually finds identical expression, signifying the fatherhood of Adam and Noah to the prediluvian and postdiluvian worlds respectively (cf. the isocolic parallels of Gen 9:1 and 1:28a: וַיְבָרֶךְ אֱלֹהִים אֶת־נֹחַ וְאֶת־בָּנָיו וַיֹּאמֶר לָהֶם פְּרוּ וּרְבוּ וּמִלְאוּ אֶת־הָאָרֶץ and וַיְבָרֶךְ אֹתָם אֱלֹהִים וַיֹּאמֶר לָהֶם אֱלֹהִים פְּרוּ וּרְבוּ וּמִלְאוּ אֶת־הָאָרֶץ).

---

[14] One exegetical implication of the correspondence between the flood and creation is the deduction of the universal dimension of the flood in the authorial conception, contrary to the local or Mesopotamian theory finding current acceptance.

[15] Cf. U. Cassuto, *From Noah to Abraham* (Jerusalem: Magnes, 1959), pp. 124–29; Westermann, *Schöpfung*, pp. 39–43.

[16] Cf. Gen 6:20 with 1:25; Gen 1:26 with 9:2 and also the divine appointment of food for man in Gen 1:29 and 9:3.

[17] The source critical attempt to distinguish the creation of the animals in Genesis 1 (attributed to P) from the second account of animal creation in Genesis 2 (attributed to J) must explain the tidy synthesis of elements of both accounts in the Noahic record within the one recreative model. Here as elsewhere the identification of form patterns calls into question the validity of the source critical method.

Genesis 9:20–27: The Fall Renewed

The structural and literary correspondence between the story of Noah's sin and the record of Adam's Fall is striking.[18] Noah's transgression[19] begins with a vineyard (Gen 9:20) while Adam's sin is set in a garden (Gen 3:1). Noah drank of the fruit of the vine while Adam ate of the fruit of the tree (Gen 9:20; 3:2), both being acts of deliberate disobedience resulting in the sinner's awareness of shameful nakedness (Gen 9:21; 3:7). While Noah's nakedness was covered by his eldest sons (Gen 9:23), Adam's nakedness was covered by God (Gen 3:32), and both the sin of Noah and the sin of Adam issued into a fearful curse and enduring division in their respective seed (Gen 9:25; 3:15). In both accounts the narrative moves from the sin of the father to the resulting blessing and cursing of the seed and finally to the genealogical development (Genesis 10 and 5). The authorial intention to relate the story of Noah's sin to Adam's Fall is literarily evident in the word-play in Gen 9:20 (cf. אִישׁ הָאֲדָמָה with אָדָם in Gen 2:7) and in the parallel of Gen 9:24 ("Noah awoke," i.e., by metonymy, his "eyes were opened," cf. Gen 3:7a).

Genesis 11–12: Renewed Conflict of the Seed

The cursing and blessing of the Adamic seed in Gen 3:15 divides the ancient world into Cainites and Sethites, according to the thematic development of Genesis 4–5. Cain, condemned to wander in the earth, founds the wicked city of Enoch to the east of Eden (Gen 7:17), an antediluvian cosmopolis finding correspondence in postdiluvian Babel on the east of the mountains of Ararat,[20] which Noah's sons found to avoid wandering in the earth (Gen 11:2, 4). The godly line of Adam is represented in the line of Seth in their collective capacity as "calling upon the name

---

[18] Cf. Cassuto, *From Noah to Abraham*, pp. 158–70 and Henry M. Morris, *The Beginning of the World* (Denver: Accent Books, 1977), pp. 125–26.

[19] The confusion in conservative commentaries is unwarranted. Noah did not discover viniculture, drinking in ignorance, being insensible to the properties of wine. Christ assured the disciples that before the flood the antediluvians were "eating and drinking" (Matt 24:38, cf. 11:19), and we may be sure that Noah both knew of wine and that his sin was deliberate.

[20] This interpretation assumes that the מִן of מִקֶּדֶם has a directional force; cf. BDB, p. 578. Separating himself from Abraham, Lot also chose the wickedness of the east region (מִקֶּדֶם) of the land (Gen 13:11).

of the Lord" (Gen 4:26). The structural correspondence in post-diluvian Genesis is unavoidably directed toward Abram, who with his family "calls upon the name of the Lord" (cf. the corre-spondence of Gen 12:8, וַיִּקְרָא בְּשֵׁם יהוה with Gen 4:26, אָז הוּחַל לִקְרֹא בְּשֵׁם יהוה). By this precise correspondence the conclusion is irresistible that the author would have us discern the identifying continuity of Israel's patriarch with the godly Sethite community of the ancient world.

This juxtaposition of Israel and the nations as reflective of the renewed conflict of the spiritual seed[21] in postdiluvian history sets the broader context for understanding the Old Testament distinction between the elect nation and the heathen, later spiri-tualized as Zion and Babel. The character of the conflict between these seed had been the subject of the Cain and Abel story in Genesis 4; that is, the conflict is to the death (cf. again Gen 3:15), and it was the neglect of this principle in the intermarriage of the Sethites and Cainites[22] that brought the entire race under the curse and caused the overthrow of the antediluvian world.[23]

The conflict between Zion and Babel becomes a major unify-ing theme throughout the entire postdiluvian scriptural record. The building of an earthly Babel by the postdiluvian faithless brings to mind the wicked city of Cain.[24] By contrast the hope of

---

[21] The terms "Israel" and the "nations" are often used in scripture in a spiritual sense apart from ethnic significance (cf. Ps 73:1; Matt 6:32; Rom 9:6–13; etc.). As such they represent the theological distinction between the sons of God and the sons of the serpent, a conception traceable to Gen 3:15 (cf. Matt 3:7; 1 John 3:12).

[22] The narratives in Genesis are rooted in the prophetic oracles, Gen 3:15 having established the determinative enmity between these Adamic seed. The intermarriage of the sons of God with the daughters of man is a further explica-tion of the strategy of the serpent, revealed in the garden, to seduce the man (Adam) through the woman (Eve), a theologically fundamental principle in Genesis 1–7.

[23] This history perhaps explains Abraham's extreme care and explicit in-struction regarding the choice of a bride for his son Isaac (cf. Genesis 24; also Jacob in Genesis 28), and sets the theological background to the understanding of the seriousness of intermarriage with non-covenant nations (cf. Samson, Solo-mon, returned exiles; also an echo in 1 Cor 7:39).

[24] Cf. the cities of wickedness—Babel, Sodom, Pithom and Rameses, the cities of the Amorites, which like Babel, were "built up to heaven," and the Jebusite city finally overcome by David. Cf. also the titanic struggle between Jerusalem and Babylon in the latter Old Testament prophets (Jeremiah 51; Isa 21:9; Dan 1:1; Zech 2:7; Micah 4:10, etc.) and in the New Testament (1 Pet 5:13; Rev 14:8; 17:5, 18).

the heavenly city among the postdiluvian faithful brings to remembrance the heavenly expectation of Abel (cf. Heb 11:4, 13-16).[25]

Eschatological Expectation: The New Judgment

The task of this study was to demonstrate that the Genesis record of postdiluvian history is so constructed as to be an essential reduplicative chronicle of antediluvian history. Now this reduplication in Genesis carries through historically only to the fourth narrative (creation, man, sin, and the beginnings of renewed conflict of the seed), the conflict between Babel and Zion constituting the rest of the scriptural drama. But the implication of the pattern of historical presentation in Genesis requires the projection of general apostasy and cosmic judgment into postdiluvian prophecy to satisfy the pattern of parallel narratives.[26] Explicit confirmation of these expectations is found in the New Testament in Christ's speaking specifically about the "days of Noah" reappearing upon the earth,[27] and the Apostle Peter's writing of the Noahic deluge as an adumbration of the eschatological fiery catastrophe.[28] Just as the destruction of the ancient

[25] Cf. Moses' anticipation of the heavenly city in Exod 15:17, the city of God in the Zion hymns (Psalms 46, 48). Cf. also the Zion of the latter prophets Jeremiah, Isaiah, Joel, Amos, Obadiah, Micah, Zephaniah, and Zechariah and the New Testament heavenly Jerusalem (Gal 4:26; Heb 12:22; Rev 21:2).

[26] That the eschatological projection is derived from the structure of Genesis may be displayed thusly: the prediluvian models *a*, *b*, *c*, *d*, and *e* correspond to postdiluvian Genesis models *a'*, *b'*, *c'*, and *d'*. The particular identification of *e'* is implicit from an inductive study of Genesis as necessitating the elements of apostasy and cosmic judgment, points finding explicit statement outside of Genesis in Matt 24:37 and 2 Pet 3:6-7. The New Testament confirms the structure of narrative parallels derived from the Genesis material (cf. also 2 Tim 3:1-5 and 2 Pet 3:1-7).

[27] It is interesting to note that the use of Enoch's preaching of judgment to his generation is applied typologically to the wicked of this world by Jude (cf. also 1 Enoch 106 [fragment of the Book of Noah]).

[28] The "Song of Moses" in Deuteronomy 32 represents Pentateuchal expectations of apostasy and cosmic judgment, containing the lament over the spiritual harlotry of Israel which will bring about a fiery overthrow of the earth (cf. especially vv 19-22). Note that the eschatological judgment finds God taking his bow of wrath once again, with which he had figuratively destroyed the world of Noah (cf. Gen 9:12-16) and with which figuratively he will finally destroy the present world.

world ushered in the present heavens and earth, so the present world will pass away before the new heavens and earth.[29]

Conclusion

Moses writes simple stories in this book of beginnings, but they contain profound teaching. They tell of light and darkness, good and evil, of gardens and graves, life and death. In Genesis we are told of the sons of the serpent and the sons of God, of the children of darkness and the children of light. The unifying feature of all these particular stories is a structural comprehension revealing God's ordination of the historical process. The historical setting was created by the divine Word. History is created by the divine Prophecy. Consequently, the inevitability of historical direction presupposed by the eschatological structure of Genesis serves as the overarching signature of divine sovereignty in the affairs of men.

> Remember the former things long past, for I am God, and there is no other; I am God, and there is no one like Me, declaring the end from the beginning and from ancient times things which have not been done; saying, "My purpose will be established, and I will accomplish all my good pleasure."
> —Isa 46:9–10

[29] It is the expectation of the everlasting eschaton of perfect righteousness (cf. 2 Pet 3:13, Revelation 21) wherein we find the fulfillment of the messianic blessings first aroused in Gen 3:15 (cf. Heb 11:16, that from Abel to Abraham the hope of the godly seed was ever in the heavenlies).

THE HISTORY OF THE WORLD: THE MACROCOSM

The World That Was

GENESIS 1 CREATION	ADAM	FALL	CONFLICT OF SEED	GENESIS 7 JUDGMENT
1. Waters of chaos cover the earth, Gen 1:1–2	1. Man commissioned in God's image, Gen 1:26	1. Adam sins in a garden, Gen 3:2	1. Cain, condemned to wander, founds wicked city of Enoch, Gen 4:17	1. Days of Noah are upon the earth, Gen 6:13
2. Spirit hovers upon face of the waters, Gen 1:2	2. Man commanded to fill the earth, Gen 1:28	2. Adam partakes of fruit of knowledge, Gen 3:6	2. Seth, with son Enosh, begins to call upon Name of LORD, Gen 4:26	2. God brings cloud upon earth to destroy the wicked with a flood, Gen 7:23
3. Dry land emerges, vegetation brought forth, Gen 1:12	3. God brings animals to Adam for naming, Gen 2:19	3. Adam shamefully naked, Gen 3:7	3. Daughters of man taken to wife by sons of God, Gen 6:2	3. Old heavens and earth pass away before the present heavens and earth, 2 Pet 3:5–7
4. Old world finished, God rests, Gen 2:2		4. Adam's nakedness covered by God, Gen 3:21		
		5. Adam's sin brings curse upon seed, Gen 3:15		

The World That Now Is

GENESIS 8 THE NEW CREATION	NOAH, THE NEW ADAM	THE FALL RENEWED	SEED CONFLICT RENEWED	REVELATION 22 THE NEW JUDGMENT
1. Waters of Noah cover the earth, Gen 7:18–19	1. Man recommissioned in God's image, Gen 9:6	1. Noah sins in a vineyard, Gen 9:20	1. Noah's sons, to avoid wandering, found wicked city of Babel, Gen 11:4	1. "Days of Noah" again upon the earth, Matt 24:37–39
2. Dove "hovers" upon face of the waters, Gen 8:9	2. Man commanded to fill the earth again, Gen 9:7	2. Noah partakes of fruit of vine, Gen 9:20	2. Shem's descendant Abram begins to call upon Name of LORD, Gen 12:8	2. God comes in clouds to destroy the wicked with a fire, Matt 24:30; cf. 2 Pet 3:7
3. Olive leaf betokens emergence of dry land, Gen 8:11	3. God brings animals to Noah for delivering, Gen 7:15	3. Noah shamefully naked, Gen 9:21	3. The harlot Babel seduces the sons of Zion throughout the ages, cf. Dan 1:1; Isa 47:1–15; Rev 17–18	3. Present heavens and earth pass away before the new heavens and earth, 2 Pet 3:13
4. Present world finished; God receives sacrifice of rest, Gen 8:21		4. Noah's nakedness covered by sons, Gen 9:23		
		5. Noah's sin brings curse upon seed, Gen 9:25		

3 | The Creator God As Cosmic Redeemer

The creative-redemptive relationship between protology and eschatology is extensively developed in the New Testament[1] as the divine work of redemption is described in the language of creation.[2] John, for example, begins his account of the new creation after the fashion used by Moses to describe the old creation (cf. ἐν ἀρχῇ, "in the beginning" found in John 1:1 and the LXX of Gen 1:1), while Paul characterizes salvation as the shining forth of the Light of Life into the heart of darkness, resulting in a new creation (2 Cor 4:6; 5:17, καινὴ κτίσις). This chapter proposes to investigate the doctrine of creation as it instructs regarding redemption.[3] Consideration will first be given to the pattern of cosmic creation in Genesis. Redemptive reenactments of this pattern throughout the scripture will then be considered.

The Pattern of Cosmic Redemption Established by the Creation

The original creation of the world, recounted in Gen 1:1-2:4, describes a processive subduing of darkness and deep, thereby

[1] The relationship between creation and redemption is primarily soteriological. From his perspective of the Old Testament, Gerhard von Rad stated that protology is soteriology; cf. "The Problem of Creation-Faith in the O.T.," in *The Problem of the Hexateuch and Other Essays*, trans. E. W. Trueman Dilken (Edinburgh and London: Oliver and Boyd, 1966), pp. 136-43. The New Testament scholar Geerhardus Vos observed likewise that soteriology is eschatology; cf. *The Pauline Eschatology* (Grand Rapids: Baker, 1979 reprint), pp. 42-61.

[2] The Old Testament likewise appealed to the creative power of God to urge confidence in divine redemption, an argument from protology to eschatology expressed in Isaiah's word from God, "I am the first, I am also the last," (Isa 48:12-14). In this context the prophet comforts God's captive people with the assurance that God's hand, which spread out the heavens, is the same hand that shall be against the Chaldeans (cf. also Psalms 74, 136).

[3] Theological redemption fundamentally implies the payment of a ransom (cf. the λύτρον word group). In a derived sense, however, the force of redemption is simply the exertion of divine effort, the making known of God's strength. In such a sense God's effort (creative effort also) is regarded as the "price," (cf. Leon Morris, *The New Bible Dictionary*, s.v. "Redeemer, Redemption" [Grand Rapids: Eerdmans, 1962] ed. J. D. Douglas, p. 1079). For creation as an act of salvation cf. Ps 74:12-17.

constituting the earth a suitable habitation (cf. Isa 45:18).[4] The Genesis account of the origin of the world is unique among ancient cosmogonies due to the absence of any suggestion of mythological conflict.[5] The creative process transforming chaos into cosmos is effected irresistibly by the Word of God without the barest hint of cosmic struggle, the *sine qua non* of mythological epic. The Genesis revelation, then, is profoundly consistent with the broader monotheistic affirmation of holy scripture.

To the mythological mind of the ancients, however, this method of creation suggested themes common to pagan cosmogonies, which, in spite of theological corruption and geographical and linguistic diffusion, are nevertheless remarkable for their structural commonality.[6] After comparing the cosmogonic myths from India, Sumer, Mesopotamia, Anatolia, Greece, and Canaan, Mary Wakeman[7] concluded that the essential elements are virtually identical. In these ancient myths, chaos is generally personified as an anti-creative monster whose defeat by the heroic god results in a regulated cosmos. The hero-god, consequent to his creative victory over the forces of chaos, establishes a royal residence from which he exercises his sovereignty in preserving cosmic order. This pattern of victory over draconic chaos followed by temple building is fundamental to the epic cosmogonies of the ancient Near East.

The monotheistic authors of scripture reformulated the Mosaic creation account at least five times in the Old Testament through the paradigm of cosmogonic polemic.[8] The creation of the world is mythologized through imagery borrowed

---

[4] As cosmogony, cf. Moses in Gen 2:4 and Ps 90:2.

[5] Attempts to infuse the Genesis record with such notions (cf. the identification of תְּהוֹם with *tiʾamat*), are strained, reflecting the presuppositions of much of modern scholarship after Gunkel regarding revelation, date, etc. (cf. Alexander Heidel, *The Babylonian Genesis* [Chicago: University of Chicago, 1951], pp. 98–101).

[6] This commonality has been the basis for the science of *Religionsgeschichte*. The method of this critical school, however, employed very definite theoretical presuppositions regarding revelation and dating of the material, necessarily at such a point proceeding from science to speculation. Biblical presuppositions (likewise theoretical) often lead to a chronological reversal of the conclusions of criticism.

[7] *God's Battle with the Monster: A Study in Biblical Imagery* (Leiden: E. J. Brill, 1973).

[8] That is, the imagery, but not the theology, was employed by the Hebrews from Semitic mythologies (cf. John L. McKenzie, "A Note on Psalm 73 [74]:13–15," *Theological Studies* 2 [1950] 281.

from related cultures as God is depicted doing battle with the dragon.[9] The redemptive pattern throughout the scripture conforms to this same epic ideology of divine victory over the anti-creative beast followed by the establishment of a royal residence or temple.[10] This pattern will be considered in six great redemptive reenactments of creation. First, the macrocosm is redeemed through the flood of Noah (the defeat of Leviathan and the establishment of the paleocosmic temple) and by the fire of the Last Day (the defeat of the man of sin and the purification of the neocosmic temple). Second, the microcosm (Israel) is redeemed at the first exodus (the defeat of pharaonic Rahab and the erection of the tabernacle) and the second exodus (the renewed defeat of Rahab and the erection of the second temple). Finally, the first Advent (the defeat of the serpent and the raising of the Temple of Christ's body) and the second Advent (the defeat of the beast from the sea and the raising of the temple-church) reenact creation.

Macrocosmic Reenactments of Creation

The Apostle Peter described two recreations of the cosmic order (2 Pet 3:5–13), the first out of the flood of Noah and the second out of the fire of the day of God.

The deliverance of the earth from the waters of the flood so closely parallels the story of the original creation that the flood narrative is often subordinated to the creation narrative in the theological synthesis of the wisdom school (cf. Pss 74:12–17; 104:9; Job 38:4–11). Nevertheless, the essential elements of epic creation do appear. In the complex of the redemptive deeds of Yahweh celebrated in Ps 74:12–17,[11] the victory over Leviathan, which results in the establishment of earth's boundaries, the restraint of the waters, and the appointing of summer and winter comports most easily with the language of the flood narrative (cf. Ps 74:15–17 with Gen 8:21–22, and Psalm 93). Likewise, Psalm

---

[9] The anti-creative monster, as Leviathan or Rahab, cf. Job 26:13; Pss 74:13–14; 89:10; Isa 27:1; 51:9.

[10] Meredith G. Kline, *The Structure of Biblical Authority* (Grand Rapids: Eerdmans, 1971), p. 79.

[11] In this passage the redemptive deeds (the plural is significant) of *Urgeschichte* and *Heilsgeschichte* are paralleled, that is, macrocosmic and microcosmic redemption is celebrated (cf. H.-J. Kraus, *Psalmen*, vol. 2 [BKAT; Neukirchen-Vluyn: Neukirchener Verlag, 1961/1978], pp. 681–82).

29 celebrates the Kingship of the Lord displayed by the flood (v 10)[12] and celebrated in his temple (v 9). In short, the wicked generation of Noah was destroyed by the waters of chaos. God, in ruling over and restraining these mighty waters, reestablished creative order in a cleansed cosmos.

The consummation of macrocosmic redemption is anticipated in the Olivet discourse (cf. Matt 24:15, the "abomination causing desolation" in the temple typically foreshadowing the end of the age)[13] and in the second Thessalonian epistle as the man of sin (the heir of all scriptural chaos figures), who would defile the cosmic temple of God, is destroyed by the Word of God, resulting in a new creation (2 Thess 2:3-8). As the Word of God in the beginning had subdued the darkness and deep, establishing the old heavens and earth, and the Voice of the Lord had ruled over the flood (cf. Ps 29:3) to constitute the present heavens and earth, so the Word of God in the consummation will subdue the beast, confirming the new heavens and earth.

Microcosmic Reenactments of Creation

By introducing the scriptural history of Israel with Genesis, Moses identifies Yahweh of the exodus with Elohim of creation.[14] Consequently the exodus-eisodus history of the hexateuch is so structured as to be a redemptive reenactment of creation.[15] The redemptive creation of Israel at the sea[16] is cast in the same narrative style of original creation as the pillar of divine presence

---

[12] מַבּוּל (cf. Gen 6:17; 7:6, 9, 11), the natural chaos power (the heavenly ocean), destroyed the historical chaos powers (the generation of Noah).

[13] The creative-redemptive epic underlies the typical significance of the temple cleansing episodes recorded in all four Gospel narratives (cf. John 2:13-17; Matt 21:12-13; Mark 11:15-17; Luke 19:45-46; also Mal 3:1-3).

[14] The inscripturation of the creation account was *ex eventu* from the perspective of the Red Sea, so the Mosaic record of creation is chronologically but not logically precedent to the record of redemption from Egypt.

[15] This theme is elaborately developed by Meredith G. Kline in *Images of the Spirit* (Grand Rapids: Baker, 1980), pp. 13-42.

[16] The Red Sea event may be understood as a polemic against the Canaanite Baal-Zaphon cosmogony (cf. Exod 14:2), wherein Baal (the fresh water creative deity) split open the sea deity Yamm (the salt water anti-creative serpent) thereupon building his northern palace (Zaphon) in celebration (cf. Otto Eissfeldt, "Baal Zaphon, Zeus Kasios und der Durchzug der Israeliten durchs Meer," *Beiträge zur Religionsgeschichte des Altertums* 1 [1932]). Pharaoh, who would hinder the creation of Israel, is called Rahab in Isa 54:5.

brings light into darkness (Exod 13:21, cf. the first creative day), the waters are divided (Exod 14:21, cf. the second creative day), and the dry land emerges (Exod 14:29, cf. the third creative day).[17] In the wilderness the superintending care of God at the creation of Israel is paralleled to the Spirit hovering over the waters of chaos (cf. רָחַף in Gen 1:2 and Deut 32:11), while the exodus event culminates in the eisodus into the paradisical Canaan, a redemptive correlative to the creative sabbath (cf. Heb 4:3–10). The redemptive pattern of victory over the chaos beast followed by the building of a cosmic sanctuary is precisely the paradigm of the Song of the Sea in Exod 15:1–18.[18] More broadly, the same paradigm is expressed in the Sinaitic covenant deliverance from Egyptian bondage and the erection of the tabernacle of the testimony.[19]

The deliverance of captive Israel from the bondage of Shinar is described by the prophets as a second exodus. Isaiah colors the promised deliverance after the epic language of the first exodus from Egypt, as a new victory over the mighty waters (תְּהוֹם רַבָּה, Isa 51:10), a second prevailing over Rahab (cf. Isa 51:9–11). The erection of the second temple follows God's ordaining of a second exodus through Cyrus (cf. Haggai, Zephaniah, Ezra, and Nehemiah).

Neocosmic Reenactments of Creation

Redemptive reenactments of the original creation follow the adventual appearances of Christ. The institution of the New

[17] Similarities with the Noahic recreation and the Jordan crossing are likewise apparent; cf. Gen 8:9 and Josh 3:13. Perhaps also Gen 6:4 and Num 13:33.

[18] Apocalyptic Daniel follows the same scheme as the creative week becomes the pattern for the redemption of the Holy Place (9:24). The Apocalypse of John describes redemption as seven plagues giving victory over the beast of the sea (13:1–6), whereupon the redeemed sing the "song of Moses" (15:3–4) as the heavenly temple is opened (15:5–8). Further, the Ezekiel pattern of the defeat of Gog and Magog and the description of the cosmic sanctuary (Ezekiel 36–46) is reflected in Revelation 20–22, likewise with the defeat of Gog and Magog followed by the description of the cosmic sanctuary.

[19] The introduction to the Davidic Covenant in 2 Samuel 7 is similarly cast in the redemptive pattern of victory over enemies followed by the erection of a royal residence. When David was given rest from his enemies, he turned his attention to the building of a temple in Zion that the Lord might dwell in the midst of his people. It was in this providential context of the house of David (cf. Psalms 89, 132) that God ordained the redemptive pattern for the true David who would defeat cosmic chaos, and the true Solomon, who would build the cosmic temple

Covenant at the First Advent is stylized by the evangelists as a new creation, occasioning striking correspondences between the Passion Week of the Gospels (cf. ἐξ ἡμερῶν in John 12:1) and the creative week of Genesis.

On the first day of the redemptive week, the Light of the World approached the temple[20] from the direction of the eastern sunrise (cf. Matt 21:9; Ps 118:26-27). During the week the Word of God spoke daily in the temple (Luke 19:47), entering into creative combat with the religious and political leaders who represented, according to John, the darkness of original creation (John 1:5, cf. 13:30). On the sixth day of Passion Week, the Word surveyed his redemptive work and pronounced it finished (John 19:30, cf. Gen 2:3), resting on the sabbath day in the rest of death (John 19:31). Thus is the old creation redemptively reenacted in the new creation.

The *logion* of Christ regarding the destruction of the earthly temple (Mark 14:58; John 2:19) and the raising of a spiritual temple[21] (Christ as the Chief Cornerstone) conforms to the redemptive pattern of victory over the beast[22] followed by the building of a cosmic temple.[23] Likewise the Second Advent of Christ (coincident with the eschatological macrocosmic redemption described above, cf. also 2 Thess 2:3-8) involves the ultimate defeat of the beast (cf. Revelation 13-15)[24] and the establishment of the eternal (neocosmic) temple.[25]

(cf. R. A. Carlson, *David, the Chosen King*, trans. Eric J. Sharpe and Stanley Rudman [Uppsala: Almquist & Wiksell, 1964] p. 98).

[20] Since creation is often described as a dwelling place that God has built (cf. Ps 104; Job 9:8; Isa 40:22) the temple represents the cosmos (cf. Ps 78:69; John 2:21; 1 Cor 6:19). The temple (as a dwelling place of the Spirit) is consequently a metaphor equally apt for macrocosmic and microcosmic expression.

[21] The conformity of scripture to the epic pattern of victory and temple building is further substantiated in that every instance of tabernacle-temple erection undertaken in the Bible finds the edifice built of victory plunder. It is so with the the tabernacle of Moses (cf. Exod 12:35-36), the temple of Solomon (1 Chr 26:27), the temple of Zerubbabel (Ezra 6:3-5), and the eschatological temple (cf. the gospel announcement in Hag 2:7, cf. Matt 12:29).

[22] The redemptive work of Christ is described as conflict with the dragon in Rev 12:7-9 and 20:1-3.

[23] The church corporately is described as a spiritual temple in New Testament theology (cf. Eph 2:21-22; 1 Pet 2:4-6).

[24] Christ, the greater than Solomon, builds his eternal temple of his saints who overcome (cf. Rev 3:12; 1 Pet 2:5).

[25] It is striking that the word "baptism" occurs with reference to the macrocosmic redemption of the flood (1 Pet 3:20-21), the microcosmic redemption of

EXCURSUS

The Pattern of Anthropological Redemption

The redemption of man (as a microcosmic temple, cf. 1 Cor 6:19) constitutes a major aspect of Pauline theology (cf. Rom 8:23), a concept derived by the apostle from Gen 2:7 (cf. 1 Cor 15:45–49). As man has borne the image of the earthly (Adam), so he will bear the image of the heavenly (Christ). These concepts will be considered in turn.

Man in the Image of Earth

The eschatological redemption of the earth and man is anticipated in the protological creation of man from the earth.[26] The תּוֹלְדוֹת pattern ("these are the generations of . . . ") first applied to the earth bringing forth Adam (created of dust) establishes the biblical image of mother earth as a womb (cf. Job 1:26; Ps 139:15). In Pauline theology the eschatological consummation is expressed in terms of the travail of the earth in childbirth, the resurrection of the last day becoming the final cosmic תּוֹלְדוֹת, when the earth brings forth the sons of God (redeemed from dust, Rom 8:22).

Man in the Image of Heaven

The spiritual redemption of man constitutes a transformation of man into the image of the heavenly (a cosmic pattern

---

the exodus (1 Cor 10:2), and the neocosmic redemption of the cross (Mark 10:38; Luke 12:50).

[26] The chthonic origin of Adam accounts for the interplay of imagery between man and the earth in scripture. Consequently when man transgresses, the earth is cursed (cf. Gen 3:17; 4:11), and only when man obeys may blessing be restored (cf. Gen 5:29). This identification of man and earth is comprehensively demonstrated in the judgment pronouncement in Gen 6:13. It is illustrated in the Mosaic covenant, for the disobedience of Israel defiles the land, while obedience blesses it (cf. Lev 18:24–28; Deuteronomy 28). Both the nation Israel and the land of Canaan must observe sabbath (Lev 25:1–22). Furthermore, the works of man are variously styled thorns, thistles, or fruit (cf. Heb 6:8; Gal 5:22), while his nature is modeled after the various types of soil in the parable of the sower (cf. Matt 13:18–23).

originally reflected in the prelapsarian earth).[27] Consequently as man was created in the image of the earthly, in redemption he is recreated in the image of the heavenly (1 Cor 15:49). This heavenly image is revealed in scripture through the metaphor of the tabernacle-temple, the appointment of which is a reflection of the heavenly order itself (cf. Heb 8:4–5).[28] Therefore, the fitting of the man of faith into a dwelling for the Spirit[29] constitutes a redemptive recreation after the norm of the heavenly pattern. The temple imagery applied by the New Testament to the church (corporately and individually) represents this redemptive transformation into the heavenly image.[30] The parallels are instructive.[31] In the innermost recesses of the temple were found the tables of the law written with the finger of God. Likewise under the New Covenant God writes his law upon the heart of the man of faith (Jer 31:33).

As the temple was the site of acceptable sacrifice, so the believer is to become a living sacrifice (Rom 12:1), a priest whose duty is to sacrifice the old nature (Rom 8:13), to petition and to praise God (Heb 13:15). The river of paradise issued forth from the throne of the eschatological temple (Ezek 47:1–12). Likewise

[27] The heavenly Glory was the archetypical pattern for the original creation. Cf. Meredith G. Kline, *Images of the Spirit*, pp. 17–26. In the eschaton the Edenic heavenly cosmos is recreated in the redemption of the earth (cf. the cosmographical correspondences between Eden [Genesis 2] and Zion [Revelation 21–22]).

[28] The heavenly pattern associated with God's dwelling place is the significance of the Hebrew word מִשְׁפָּט, and as such it was reflected in the tabernacle (Exod 26:30), the temple of Solomon (1 Kgs 6:38), and the eschatological temple of Ezekiel (Ezek 42:11). The Servant of the Lord shall arrange the earth after this pattern (Isa 42:4, cf. Eph 1:10).

[29] In this sense the "indwelling" of the Spirit is an eschatological expression (John 7:39; 14:17), appropriate under the Old Covenant only locally (with reference to the Zion temple, cf. John 4:21). Under the New Covenant after Pentecost, however, it is applied universally (with reference to the believer, cf. John 4:23–24 and Eph 1:13; 2:22; 1 Cor 6:19). Nowhere in the Old Testament is Israel styled the temple of God as is the church in the New Testament.

[30] The redemptive pattern of creation out of darkness and constitution of a temple is presupposed. Cf. Paul in 2 Corinthians 4–5. God commanded light to shine into our darkness (4:6), whereupon we wait to be tabernacled upon from above (5:1–3).

[31] These parallels suggest the pattern for spiritual maturity, both in regard to the believer and to the church. The more accurately the Christian and the Church conform to the pattern of the temple (the site of acceptable worship), the more perfectly does the work of the Spirit find expression.

the Spirit flows forth abundantly from the innermost being of the
Christian like a river of living water (John 7:38-39).[32]

[32] Other parallels, perhaps less certain, are still interesting. The robes of the
priest suggest the heavenly pattern (cf. Meredith G. Kline, *Images of the Spirit*,
pp. 42-47). The man of faith subsists upon the hidden manna (Rev 2:17). His
prayers ascend like the incense (cf. Rev 8:3-4), his witness is like the candlestick
(Rev 1:20). He is gifted of the Spirit for the fitting of the church (Eph 4:11-16), as
had been Bezalel and Oholiab for the tabernacle of Moses (Exod 31:1-11) and
Hiram the coppersmith for the temple of Solomon (1 Kgs 7:13-14).

4 | The First Adam and the Last Adam

The orderliness and goodness of God's creative work in Gen 1:1-2:4 suggest a divine teleology of creation, that is, a broader basis of purposive history. The goal of the historical process initiated in Gen 1:28 is a world subdued by and filled of man. Only such a world will satisfy the requirements of God's command. This command is two-fold (1) Adam is to be fruitful, to fill the earth, and (2) Adam is to subdue the created order to his dominion. Both the woman and the animals are brought into Adam's sphere of sovereignty, the woman to enable Adam to be fruitful, and the animals that Adam might exercise his rule. The entrance of sin and death, however, constitute an antithetical challenge to the divine command, for the serpent, which should have submitted to the woman (Gen 1:26, 28), rules over her. The woman, who was to bring life to Adam, brings him death. Consequently the work of Adam is rendered vain (cf. Psalm 90; Qoh 1:2-3; Rom 8:20). Because of the Fall man becomes powerless to obey God's command. Man's labor of subduing the earth becomes wearisome, and woman's labor of filling the earth becomes sorrowful (Gen 3:16-19a). Instead of subduing the creation for God, Adam is himself made subject to the creation by Satan (cf. Rom 5:12). Instead of begetting children unto life, Adam can bring forth only sons of death (cf. 1 Cor 15:22). The problem is thus posed: does the entrance of sin and death into human history subvert the first and primary purpose of God for man? Does Gen 1:28 represent the only design of the Creator God for his creation not finding historical actualization, and that very good? Is the command of the Creator for man rendered vain?

The scriptural teaching making possible a reconciliation of the question of God's sovereignty and the divine *telos* of history, as it finds especial development in the New Testament, is the hope of the resurrection, the consummating work of the new Man, the last Adam. It is Christ in his sinless humanity who is

27

obedient to the divine command. Adam's physical commission was typically ordained to set forth the spiritual commission of the true Adam (cf. 1 Cor 15:45-49). Thus it is Christ in whose work history again finds meaningful process (Isa 53:11), and it is he in whose person history finds ultimate fulfillment (Eph 1:10). The one who tasted death will bring many sons to glory (Heb 2:10); the one who was put to grief will have dominion over all things (Ps 110:2; 1 Cor 15:25-26). The first Adam had been given a bride by the Father that he might fill the earth with physical sons. The last Adam is given the church as a bride by the Father (Eph 5:23-32) that the earth might be filled with spiritual sons. The first Adam had been subdued by the serpent. The last Adam rules over the serpent in gaining dominion over all things (Rev 12:1-9). The *Protevangelion* of Gen 3:15 is thus the promise of purposive history, that the righteous Seed would subdue. Redemptive history, then, finds consummation in the resurrection of the last day. Christ, who is true Man, through the resurrection will raise many to life, filling the earth by subduing death, the last enemy. Then is the divine command to man fulfilled in history, and God is all in all (1 Cor 15:28).

The thesis of this chapter is that in the divine command man is commissioned to reproduce God's own activity in creation, that is, to subdue and to fill the earth. Contextually then, the divine image is the anthropological enablement for obedience to the divine command. After the disobedience of the first Adam, however, the divine command (as restated in the *Protevangelion*) is confirmed through the divine covenants to Noah, Abraham, and David. Each of these promissory covenants successively designates more specifically the Seed who would subdue the earth. Christ, who is the Seed promised as well as the Mediator of the New Covenant, expresses in the Great Commission the redemptive correlative to the divine command, namely, that the earth is to be filled with disciples and subdued unto obedience to the Word. Finally, the resurrection becomes the *telos* of history whereby the divine command finds consummation.

The task of this study is to demonstrate that Christ, as true Man in the divine image, fulfills the divine command in filling and subduing the earth. Accordingly, the first part of this study traces the scriptural republication of the divine command expressed through the covenants of promise issuing into the Seed who would subdue. The second part of this study presents a contextual argument for the identification of the divine image (as presuppositional to the divine command) finding perfect expression in Christ. Finally, the last part of the study presents an argument from scripture for the work of Christ historically satisfying the requirements of the divine command.

The Covenants of Promise

The divine command (or creative mandate) originally pronounced to Adam—that he should fill the earth and rule over the beast (Gen 1:28)—is formalized covenantally through three administrations (i.e., three mediators: Noah, Abraham, and David) in postdiluvian history prior to the ratification of the New Covenant in the blood of Christ. Each of these covenants, though administratively and typically diverse, is nevertheless an expression of the same promise that a Seed would come who should subdue the earth. Each is progressively more particularistic in defining the Seed: the Noahic identifying the Semitic race, the Abrahamic identifying the Israelite nation, and the Davidic identifying the family of Jesse. Yet each is equally universalistic in scope, encompassing every creature (Noah), all nations (Abraham), and all the realms (David). These covenants as republications of the divine command will be considered in turn.

The benedictory pronouncement to Adam in Gen 1:28 finds virtually precise restatement to Noah in Gen 9:1-2.[1] In Gen 6:18[2] God promises to establish his covenant with Noah through the saving of his seed[3] and the deliverance of the animals in the ark. Noah, as mediator of the covenant, promises continuance of blessing through Shem (Gen 9:26), in whose tent Japheth would dwell and Canaan would serve (Gen 9:25-27). The covenant finds continuance with Abraham in Gen 12:1-3.[4] Once again the

---

[1] Cf. Gen 9:1-2, "Be fruitful and multiply, and fill the earth. And the fear of you and the terror of you shall be on every beast of the earth and on every bird of the sky; with everything that creeps on the ground, and all the fish of the sea, into your hand they are given" with Gen 1:28, "Be fruitful and multiply, and fill the earth, and subdue it; and rule over the fish of the sea and over the birds of the sky, and over every living thing that moves on the earth."

[2] This is the first use of the word "covenant" in scripture.

[3] Cf. Heb 11:7; 1 Pet 3:20.

[4] This passage is the fundamental statement of the Abrahamic covenant (cf. Gal 3:16; Acts 3:25).

expectation is of a Seed[5] who would subdue the earth by ruling over the nations cursing Abraham and prospering those blessing him.[6] Likewise, the Davidic covenant expressed in 2 Sam 7:8-17[7] anticipates a Davidic Seed who should rule the earth (cf. Pss 72:8-11; 89:25-27) and subdue his enemies (cf. Pss. 89:23; 110:1-2, 5-6; 132:18).

The concerns of the divine command restated in the covenants of promise find final expression in the New Covenant. Christ, as the Elohim of creation, appears to the disciples after the resurrection.[8] As God breathed the breath of life into Adam, so Christ breathed the Spirit of Life into the disciples (cf. ἐμφυσάω in the LXX of Gen 1:7 and John 20:22). In the Johannine context this creative reenactment is subsequent to the commissioning of the disciples after the divine command (expressed in John 20:21). Consequently the Great Commission (cf. Matt 28:19-20; Luke 24:47) is the redemptive correlative to the divine command. The redemptive mandate of the last Adam, the Mediator of the New Covenant, expresses the concerns typified by all the covenants of promise; namely, that (1) all the earth should be filled with Christ's disciples, and that (2) they, like Adam, should observe God's commandments, in this way subduing the serpent who counsels disobedience (cf. Rom 16:20).

The Divine Image

The apex of God's creative activity is reached in Gen 1:26-27, in which the divine counsel resolves to create man in God's own "image and likeness" (צֶלֶם and דְּמוּת).[9] Lacking any specific

---

[5] The Abrahamic covenant particularizes the seed through Isaac, the son of promise. Yet ultimately the expression anticipates Christ (cf. Gal 3:16).

[6] Thus the Gospel is preached in Genesis (cf. Gal 3:8).

[7] This is the formal statement of a covenant, though the designation is applied only afterwards (cf. Pss 89:3; 132:12). The likelihood of a covenant with Adam, though not in Genesis so designated (cf. Hos 6:7?), must then be allowed. Further evidence of a creative covenant with Adam is suggested by (1) Gen 6:18, the covenant with Noah is confirmed rather than initiated (i.e., הֲקִים not כָּרַת) and (2) Rom 5:12, the theology requiring a "federal" headship for Adam (cf. *foedus*, covenant).

[8] Resurrection Sunday, the first day of the week of the new creation, witnesses the last Adam undertaking the work of the first Adam as he begins to fill and subdue the earth.

[9] This expression is the heart of theological anthropology. This compound, a nominal hendiadys composed of equivalent terms linked for emphasis, finds

textual explication of the expression, a contextual reconstruction out of the creation account is the only approach by which we are likely to understand the nature of man as "image."[10] Consequently, the method of this discussion will be to examine the creation account in order to discern predications of God paralleled by similar predications about man. The position of this study is that in his "image" man reflects God both in his person and in his work.[11] As the first Adam bore the "image of the earthly," so the last Adam bears the "image of the heavenly" (1 Cor 15:49). Thus it is in the Lord Christ, the true Adam, that the "image" finds final realization (1 Cor 4:4; Col 1:15).

First, man is in the earthly image of God in his person. The revelation of God in Genesis 1 is preeminently that of a communicative God. The divine, creative purpose is accomplished through the medium of the Word (cf. John 1:1-14). God speaks, and it is significant that he uniquely endows his image so as to permit man to speak after him. Just as God had demonstrated his dominion over the various members of creation by naming them (cf. Gen 1:5), so he brings the animals to Adam, permitting his image thus to exercise dominion by giving names (Gen 2:19). Thus in the exercise of ruling with the word, man reflects his Creator.

Second, man is in the earthly image of God in his work. The pattern of God's work during the six creative days is essentially twofold. During the first three days God is presented as subduing the chaos of original creation, bringing about an ordered cosmos. During the final three days God is depicted as filling the heavens and the earth, the former with the starry hosts and the latter with all manner of animate life. The cycle of divine work concludes with six days, and God rests from work on the seventh day. The work of man, as he is commissioned by his Creator, is a mirror image of the divine activity in Genesis 1. Man is commanded to

---

binary parallelism in Gen 1:26 and 1:27 (cf. the singular, but wholly sufficient use of "image" found in Gen 9:6).

[10] Cf. L. Köhler, *Theologie des Alten Testaments* (Tübingen: J. C. B. Mohr, 1947), p. 133.

[11] Any theological statement must reckon with the Fall of man insofar as it affects the original image, for though the New Testament agrees with the Old Testament that the image survives in postlapsarian man (cf. Gen 9:6, and "likeness" in James 3:18), nevertheless in a true soteriological sense it must be renewed (Rom 8:29; 2 Cor 3:18; Col 3:10). Christian theology must likewise consider the image in its spiritual as well as physical signification (1 Cor 15:49).

fill the earth and to subdue the creation (Gen 1:28). He is granted six days in which to work and provided with a sabbath for rest from work.[12] Thus in his work of filling and subduing within the weekly cycle man is commissioned in the image of his Maker.

Christ, however, as the God-man, is in the heavenly image of God in his person as the incarnate Word. John, the evangelist, presents Christ as the incarnate Logos (John 1:1, 14a). He is the One who communicates the Father, being himself the visible image of the invisible God (John 1:18; cf. Paul in Col 1:15). Just as God spoke through the written Word, so he has spoken through the living Word (Heb 1:1–3). Through his Word, Christ exercises dominion over both natural (Luke 8:24–25) and spiritual (Matt 8:16; 2 Thess 2:8) chaos powers. Through his Word, he gives life to spiritual sons (John 5:24; James 1:18; 1 Pet 1:23).

Christ likewise expresses the heavenly image of God in His work: filling, subduing, and resting. The last Adam fills the earth by redeeming the sons of the first Adam. As true Man he is the Redeemer (גֹּאֵל) who delivers his human kinsmen (cf. Isa 59:20). He is the firstborn among many brethren destined to be conformed to his image (Rom 8:29). Hence he is likewise the near kinsman (*levir*) who raises up seed from the sons of death, imparting an everlasting name to those cut off without seed (Isa 56:4–5). Christ now subdues the earth through the spiritual conflict he sustains with Satan.[13] In the Old Testament mythopoeic language is used to describe the work of the Father during the creation week in subduing the chaos beast under the figure of the dragon. The Hebrew poets describe God's creation with the borrowed imagery of mythical cosmogonies from cognate cultures depicting the grand conflict between chaos and cosmos.[14] The Rahab-Dragon motif appears in Job 26:12–13 and Ps 89:10–11

---

[12] Cf. the generic nature of the Sabbath in Mark 2:27; the Sabbath was made for man.

[13] E. Jacob is quite helpful here: "Dominion through struggle reproduces God's own action: the earliest traditions about creation of which we have traces in certain poetic texts represent it as a struggle and victory of Yahweh over the power of chaos," and further, "From the serpent of Genesis to the beasts of Daniel, the forces of evil are symbolized by animal powers; and this is why we think that the image of God as dominion over the animals also implies to some extent dominion over evil" (*Theology of the Old Testament*, trans. A. W. Heathcote and P. J. Allcock [New York: Harper and Row, 1958], p. 170).

[14] M. Wakeman, *God's Battle with the Monster, A Study in Biblical Imagery* (Leiden: E. J. Brill, 1973), p. 59.

in such contexts, and the God of creation is said to rule over the anti-creation monster by an exercise of creative fiat. Just as God is depicted as subduing the chaos dragon in the creation account, so the God-man will carry on spiritual conflict with the dragon[15] to bring about the new creation. Such imagery for eschatological conflict appears as early as Isa 27:1, being more fully developed in the Apocalypse (cf. the parallel passages in Rev 12:7–9 and 20:1–3). Moreover, the New Testament takes the physical creation of Genesis as a type of the spiritual creation of the believer (cf. John 1:4–5; 2 Cor 4:6; 5:17). Consequently, the work of Christ in redemption reproduces the work of God in creation as he delivers his people from darkness to light. The evangelist John portrays Christ in such a role as the Elohim of redemption. Just as God surveyed his work on the sixth day of creation week, concluding that all was "finished" (Gen 2:1), so Christ concluded all to be "finished" (John 19:30), whereupon he rested the seventh day in the rest of death (John 19:30–31).

In conclusion, Christ, the last Adam, is the true image of God (2 Cor 4:4). This image consists in his being the Word who works redemption (subduing and filling) and who rests from work in victory. This pattern of predicates informs the descriptions of Christ in the parallel passages of Ephesians 1 and Colossians 1, where Christ as the image of the invisible God subdues all things to himself (Eph 1:22; Col 1:20) becoming thereby the Head of the Church (Eph 1:22–23; Col 1:18). Having worked reconciliation he rests, sitting down at the right hand of the Father from whence he exercises dominion (Eph 1:20, cf. Col 1:16). The same pattern appears in Heb 1:3. Christ, the exact representation of God, upholds all things by his powerful Word (Heb 1–3a), subduing sin by making purification for his people (Heb 1:3b), and resting from work at the right hand of Majesty (Heb 1:3c). This fundamental theological affirmation of Christ as *homo imago dei* is introductory, then, to the Christologies of Ephesians, Colossians, John, and Hebrews. The God-man, the true image of the Creator in his person, is the one qualified to fulfill the divine command in his work.

---

[15] W. Foerster writes, "Δράκων, which the ancients derived from δέρκομαι, means 'serpent,' esp. 'dragon' or 'sea-monster.'" *Theological Dictionary of the New Testament*, trans. G. Bromiley (Grand Rapids: Eerdmans, 1964) vol. 2, p. 281.

The Divine Command

Consistent with the creative mandate to fill the earth, the last Adam through the redemptive mandate becomes the Father of many sons. While the metaphor of sonship is freely applied to the church in the New Testament, the customary referent in the corresponding paternal metaphor is to God the Father (so Matt 5:9; John 1:12; 1 John 3:1; Rom 8:14-17; 2 Cor 6:18; Gal 3:26). Nevertheless, the figure of Christ in his humanity as Father to the elect is not unknown, being implicitly expressed in Paul as Christ is portrayed under the aspect of his headship to the elect. As Paul develops this concept in Romans 5, he begins by asserting that Adam in his physical life was a figure of Christ in his spiritual life (Rom 5:14). As depicted by the apostle, just as Adam gave physical life to his seed (i.e., physical fatherhood), so the last Adam imparts spiritual life to his seed (i.e., spiritual fatherhood). Adam's disobedience delivered his physical posterity to condemnation. The obedience of the last Adam resulted in the deliverance of his spiritual posterity to justification. Consequently, as Adam heads a race of the rebellious, Christ heads a race of the righteous (Rom 5:19).[16]

Perhaps the most poignant development of this theme of Christ as the spiritual Father of the elect brethren is found in Luke's narrative of the Ethiopian eunuch (Acts 8). In the providence of God, Philip, the evangelist, encountered the Ethiopian as he was reading the great Servant oracle of Isaiah (52:13-53:12) and happened upon that portion describing the humiliation of Christ in his death. Isaiah had lamented, "who shall relate his generation, for his life is removed from the earth." The irony of Luke's narrative is that the eunuch was reading that portion of scripture which foresaw that Messiah would himself be cut off without physical seed. In the development of the account of the eunuch's evangelization, Luke describes a higher irony, this conversion being itself a fulfillment of that Isaianic oracle, for as the Ethiopian comes to faith the Servant "sees his seed" (Isa 53:10). Well might Luke record that the eunuch went on his way rejoicing, for Isaiah subsequently summons the barren ones to shout

---

[16] For sonship in the New Testament as a spiritual relationship, set forth in contrast to physical kinship, cf. John 1:11-13; Matt 12:46-50; Gal 3:29.

for joy for the multitude of their begetting (Isa 54:1) and comforts the eunuchs partaking of the divine covenant with the promise of an everlasting name, a memorial better than that of sons and daughters (Isa 56:3–5). The Ethiopian, then, comes to the commonwealth of the covenant through the true Abraham, the Father of a multitude. And the eunuch comes to faith as a newborn son of the true Adam, being baptized into the brotherhood of spiritual sons begotten of one Father, even Christ.

Consistent with the creative mandate to subdue the earth, the last Adam through the redemptive mandate becomes the one who has dominion. The investiture of Adam with the commission to rule (רָדָה) in Gen 1:28, the fundamental text, is most likely the basis of the metaphor for the work of the last Adam in three derived Old Testament texts. First, in the oracle of Balaam (Num 24:15–19), the hireling of Balak envisions the Christ subduing even the most recalcitrant enemies of Israel, then under the figure of Moab and Edom, concluding that the one from Jacob shall "have dominion" (רָדָה; Num 24:19, cf. Amos 9:11–12 with Acts 15:15–18). Second, the rulership of the true David is to encompass all the Gentiles, for such is the messianic expectation of Psalm 72. The psalmist promises that Christ's kingdom will extend "from the River to the ends of the earth," and that he shall "rule (רָדָה) from sea to sea" (Ps 72:8, cf. Rom 15:8–12). But perhaps the most striking use of "rule" in the Old Testament is found in Psalm 110. In this passage the Father commands the exalted Christ, the last Adam, "Rule (רָדָה) in the midst of your enemies" (Ps 110:2). The Apostle Paul cites this psalm in his remarkable discourse upon the great resurrection of the last day (1 Cor 15:25–26). He reveals that the work of Christ in the present kingdom age is a suprahistorical exercise of his dominion by subduing spiritual enemies,[17] (cf. Peter also in Acts 2:33–36). Thus, while Christ is now Ruler *de jure*, at the resurrection of the just he will be Ruler *de facto*, having destroyed death itself (cf. Heb 2:8; Col 2:15).

---

[17] Paul conceives of the present warfare as spiritual (2 Cor 10:3–5; Eph 6:12). He identifies Christ's greatest enemy as death. The church also more than conquers even in history through her King, who goes forth conquering and to conquer (Rev 6:2). The rectoral and distributive judgment upon the ungodly in history demonstrates that the indivisible, everlasting law of God (Matt 5:17–19) is continually and effectively executed by Zion's King (Psalms 2; Rev 12:5). In this sense the church is ever victorious in history, as the nations break not the law but themselves by their disobedience.

In conclusion, the divine commission to man in Genesis 1 must be fulfilled by man. Adam's disobedience subjects the creation to vanity, disqualifying both himself and his seed, for he is himself subdued of evil and can beget but sons of death (Genesis 3 and 5). Consequently, it is the last Adam, the true Man in the divine image, who comes to carry out the divine command. It is he who will subdue spiritual enemies and it is he who will see his seed (Isa 52:13–53:12). The earth, subjected momentarily to vanity, is in labor and travail, at the resurrection to bring forth a multitude of the sons of God (cf. Rom 8:20–21). The creation, upon the death of death, when the last enemy is subdued, will be redeemed from corruption in the restitution of all things (Acts 3:21). Then does the historical process find significant conclusion, the new heavens and earth, wherein righteousness dwells everlastingly, being ushered in according to His promise (2 Pet 3:13).

EXCURSUS

The Mosaic Covenant and the Law of Christ

Few controversies have so continually troubled the people of God more than the question of the relation of Moses to Christ, of the Old to the New Covenant. In the infancy of the church legalists and antinomians threatened her life, and in her maturity there are yet heretics who would return the church to the discipline of a schoolmaster on the one hand, or would impugn the law of God on the other. This discussion will approach the question by contrasting the Old and New Covenants while comparing the law of Moses and the law of Christ.

The Contrast Between the Old and New Covenants

First, Moses is not a covenant of promise. The genealogy of Christ, the promised Seed, is traceable through every covenantal administration but Moses. Consequently the Old Covenant stands very much alongside the redemptive program covenantally furthered through Adam, Noah, Abraham, and David.

Second, Moses was a covenant of bondage. The great irony of Israel's emancipation was that Moses delivered the people from

physical to spiritual bondage. Mount Sinai bears children who
are to be slaves (Gal 4:24). The law was powerless to deliver from
spiritual bondage; it awaited the true Moses who would lead
God's people to liberty (Deut 18:15). This theme is developed by
Paul in Galatians 4. The birth of Christ is the advent of the true
Moses who would redeem the slaves of Sinai (Gal 4:4–5). Christ
appeared in the fulness of time (Gal 4:4), like Moses after four
hundred years of prophetic silence and political oppression of
Israel. His life was sought by Herod, the new pharaoh who would
slay the sons of Israel that he might destroy the seed.[18] Through
the exodus of the New Covenant (cf. ἔξοδος in Luke 9:31) the true
Moses delivered his people from the spiritual bondage that the
Old Covenant could reveal but not remove.[19]

Third, Moses was not a covenant of rest. It was likewise a
great irony that the covenant of Moses, which taught so particularly about sabbath and sacrificial rest (מְנוּחָה, שַׁבָּת) could realize
neither. It is instructive that Moses can only see from a distance
the sabbath rest typified by Canaan (cf. Lev 25:2; Psalm 95;
Hebrews 4), that Moses leads the people to the land of promise,[20]
but he himself cannot enter it.[21] The true Moses, however, is
likewise the true Joshua (Greek Ἰησοῦς), and Christ leads his
people not only victoriously from bondage but also triumphantly
into their consummatory rest in paradise. Similarly, the ceaseless
cycle of Aaronic sacrifice for sin could not bring the rest it represented. The law had appointed men as high priests who were
weak (Heb 7:28), who sacrificed for their own sins as well as those
of the people. Aaron's first presiding over public worship in
Israel was the consecration of the golden calf. The longing is thus
aroused for one to come who could purify the sons of Levi[22] and

[18] Ironically, the Prince of Israel found refuge in the land of bondage, Egypt.
[19] Just as some in Israel desired to return to the bondage of Egypt (Exod 16:3),
so some in the church would return to the bondage of Sinai (Gal 4:9).
[20] Here is typified the propaedeutic character of the law (Gal 4:1–2).
[21] The transfiguration narrative demonstrates the surpassing glory of the
New to the Old Covenant. Moses is in the land on the mount of transfiguration,
but only in anticipation of the true exodus (Luke 9:31) accomplished in Jerusalem by Christ. The transfiguration of Christ graphically distinguishes the
greater glory of Christ's to Moses' radiant glory upon the mount (cf. Exod
34:29–30 with Luke 9:29, 36).
[22] So Mal 3:3 teaches of the Melchizedekian priesthood of Christ. The inability of the Mosaic covenant to redeem is further implied by the passivity of the
priest and the Levite in the parable of the Good Samaritan (Luke 10:31–32).

accomplish once for all an eternal sacrifice. The true Aaron, however, is after the order of Melchizedek, and Christ has made an eternal sacrifice in the everlasting Temple, bringing in the sacrificial rest Aaron never knew.

Fourth, Moses was a covenant of condemnation (2 Cor 3:7). Because the law was holy, it condemned sin. The covenant of Moses was thus terrible, fearsome to fallen man. Even Moses was full of trembling at the thunder of Sinai. The letter of the law knew no mercy. For ten rejections of the wrath of God evidenced in the plagues, God destroyed the Egyptians in the sea. Likewise for ten provocations of the wrath of God in the exodus, God buried the sons of Israel in the wilderness (Num 14:22). The evangelist John contrasts the significance of Moses' beginning of miracles, the changing of water into blood (a sign of death), with that of Christ, the true Moses who changes water into wine (a sign of joy, John 2:1-11). The law came by Moses, but grace and truth by Jesus Christ (John 1:17).

Fifth, Moses was a covenant of shadow. The transitory nature of the Mosaic covenant is proved by its typological character.[23] The tables of the law broken by Moses (Exod 32:19) required a restitution by God (Exod 34:1). Likewise the law of Moses broken by Israel (Jer 31:32) required a new restitution by God in the form of a New Covenant (Jer 31:33-34). The tabernacle of Moses served simply as a copy of the heavenly reality, the portable paladium in the wilderness a pale shadow of the eternal Temple upon the cosmic mountain.[24] In Christ the true Moses, however, shadow becomes reality.

The Law of Moses and the Law of Christ

First, the old commandment is the new commandment (1 John 2:7).[25] The love of God and the brethren, as the everlasting law, is the theme of 1 John. This message was taught before Moses, from the beginning; namely, that we are to love one

[23] Consequently, the covenant of Moses begins 430 years after the promise to Abraham (Gal 3:17) and ends with the promised Messiah (Gal 3:19). See also Heb 8:13, where the "old" Covenant is supplanted by the "new."

[24] The greater glory of Christ to Moses is seen in that Moses built the tabernacle copy while Christ built the cosmic house (Heb 3:3). The glory of Moses was veiled and transitory (2 Cor 3:13, 15). The glory of Christ is unveiled (2 Cor 3:14, 16) and eternal (2 Cor 3:8-11).

another, not as Cain who killed his brother (1 John 3:11-12), but as Christ, who died for his brothers. Brotherly love is the test of love for God (1 John 4:20-21; 5:2-3). It is ever so, whether the law be taught by Moses (Deut 6:5; Lev 19:18) or by Christ (Matt 22:34-40).[26]

Second, the ten words of the Mosaic covenant (Deut 4:13) are expressions of the eternal law, the foundation of cosmic order. At the center of every cosmological system God has placed the ten commandments. The tabernacle-temple is consistently a metaphor for creation whether as macrocosm (the heavens and earth, cf. Job 9:8; Psalm 104; Isa 40:22) or microcosm (man, cf. John 2:21; 1 Cor 6:19; 2 Cor 5:1). The creation of the old heavens and earth is accomplished by the ten words of God (וַיֹּאמֶר אֱלֹהִים),[27] and it is precisely this word in its legal expression that will abide into the new heavens and earth (cf. Matt 5:18; Luke 16:17). The tabernacle of the wilderness, modeled after the heavenly temple revealed at Sinai, contained at its center the tablets of the law, while the temple of Solomon, likewise reflecting the order of cosmic creation (Ps 78:69), contained as well the tablets of the ten words (1 Kgs 8:9 = 2 Chr 5:10). The church, as the eschatological temple, the foundation of the new heavens and earth (Rev 21:1-3), is built of men in whom the law is written on tablets of flesh (2 Cor 3:3).[28]

Third, the ten commandments of Sinai are the ten commandments of Zion. The New Testament contrast between Sinai and Zion (cf. Gal 4:24-26; Heb 12:18-24) is covenantal, not legal. The ten commandments engraved upon stone from the summit of Sinai are appropriate for the summit of Zion, and are placed in the ark of Solomon's temple (1 Kgs 8:9 = 2 Chr 5:10). The everlasting law expressed in thunder at Sinai was the same law celebrated in psalm at Zion (Ps 19:7-14; cf. Heb 12:18-24).

Fourth, the ten words of the Old Covenant are the ten words

[25] The law is not contrary to but according to the Gospel (1 Tim 1:8-11). The law stated by Moses was synecdoche. Its legal principles abide (cf. 1 Tim 1:9-10 with the ten commandments).

[26] That death reigned from Adam to Moses demonstrates the penal authority of the eternal law of God (cf. Rom 5:14, 1:32).

[27] Cf. Gen 1:3, 6, 9, 11, 14, 20, 24, 26, 28, 29. As God created the cosmic order with ten words, so he creates societal order with ten commandments.

[28] The law, though darkened by sin, is at the center of man as microcosm. The violation of the law of conscience written on the heart (Rom 2:15) is the ground of condemnation for those without the law of Moses (Rom 1:18-32; 2:12-16).

of the New Covenant, hence the everlasting law of God transcends the testaments (Jer 31:31-33). The Mosaic covenant required the law to be obeyed from the heart (Deut 6:6) but could provide no enablement to that obedience (Deut 5:29; 29:4). The New Covenant prophecy of Jer 31:31-33 contains the promise that the law, broken by physical Israel, will be kept by spiritual Israel through the enablement of God.[29]

Fifth, the law of Moses is the law of love, hence it is also the law of Christ (cf. Deut 6:5; Lev 19:18; Matt 22:34-40; John 13:34; 14:15; 15:10). The center of Mosaic law was the love of God and man, a principle which is the heart of the law of Christ. To the Apostle Paul, love was the fulfillment of the law of Moses (Rom 13:8-10; cf. Gal 5:13-14) and the operative principle of the law of Christ (cf. 1 Cor 9:19-23). In Rom 14:1-23 the apostle develops the preeminence of love in the interpretation of the law. Under the Old Covenant certain days were to be observed out of love for God. Under the New Covenant love of God does not allow the rejection of a brother for the observation of days. Likewise, the covenant of Moses required the eating only of clean foods out of a love for God. The covenant of Christ requires abstinence from foods giving offense to God's children.[30] The principle of love, then, is the essence of every commandment, whether of Moses or Christ. And love never fails (1 Cor 13:8).

[29] Because the New Covenant is the Everlasting Covenant (Heb 13:20) even the psalmist can rejoice in the law (Pss 37:31; 40:8; 119:11; cf. Isa 51:7) and weep at the spirit of disobedience working in his members (Ps 119:136, cf. the lament of Paul in Rom 7:22-24).

[30] Dietary law is given by God to Adam (Gen 1:29; 2:16-17), to Noah (Gen 9:3-4) and elaborately to Moses (Leviticus 11). The principle is always that obedience is based on love, whatever the command or in spite of its diversity (Rom 14:14).

5 | Judgment, Salvation and the Oracle of Destiny

Man's first disobedience in paradise was the occasion for the original prophetic oracle in Gen 3:14-19, a pronouncement of God's wrath in retribution and his mercy in restoration. This great fountainhead of judgment and salvation is a paradigm of prophetic utterance throughout the scripture, a model of all God's messages of woe and comfort.[1] The first part of this chapter will be an examination of the significance of the word of prophetic judgment as the anti-creative (*nōn fīat*) divine utterance in light of the creative (*fīat*) word of God. This definition of prophetic judgment as the chaotic word opposing the creative word occasions, however, the theological tension of an apparent dualism of equally ultimate and contradictory expressions. The second part of this chapter will attempt to demonstrate that the prophetic oracle of Gen 3:14-19 resolves this tension, consistent with the great monotheistic affirmation of holy scripture, by establishing the pattern of divine transformation of cursing into blessing, a word of prophetic salvation.

Prophetic Judgment

Prophetic utterance in scripture is far from the idle breath of man. Such a word possesses the inherent efficacy of realizing itself in history;[2] that is, history in the scripture is determined by the word. Just as the worlds were created by the divine word in the beginning, so the subsequent ages of history are created by divine prophecy. The essential divine nature of prophetic utterance is seen in its efficacious character[3] and irrevocability.[4]

---

[1] Cf. Th. Vriezen, *An Outline of Old Testament Theology* (Newton, Mass.: Charles T. Branford Company, 1970), p. 233.

[2] Cf. W. J. Moore, *A Study of the Concept of the Mighty Word in Ancient Hebrew Literature* (Chicago: The University of Chicago Libraries, 1940), p. 3.

[3] Cf. the confidence of Jacob in the power of blessing shown by his scheming (Gen 27:1-29) and wrestling (Gen 32:24-29).

[4] Both Isaac and Balaam are powerless against it (Gen 27:30-33; Num 23:20).

41

Prophetic judgment sustains an antithetically parallel relationship to the creative word, a principle clearly illustrated in Jeremiah's commissioning. The word of Yahweh comes to the prophet, appointing him to destroy and overthrow as well as to build and establish (Jer 1:4, 10). The disobedience of Judah had provoked the wrath of God, evoking the anti-creative word of prophetic judgment which, figuratively, was to reduce the kingdom and people of Judah to the chaos of Gen 1:2, an uninhabited waste and void (Jer 4:23-26).

This anti-creative aspect of biblical judgment is a consistent category of thought throughout the Old Testament. It is comprehensively illustrated in universal history by Adam and his world, and in redemptive history by David and his kingdom. Adam, in the beginning, was created of dust and appointed to rule over the earth. This dust, however, which would be like God, was judged by the Word he had disobeyed (Gen 3:19), and Adam was made dust again. Likewise the world, born of water in creation, was constituted a paradise, but when sin filled it with moral chaos the divine judgment reduced the world to water again (Gen 7:19-20). David, moreover, was taken from the sheepcotes of Bethlehem and made monarch in the city of the great King. By disobeying the word of God with the wife of Uriah, however, David provoked the word of divine judgment (2 Sam 12:10-12), and the house of David was reduced to obscurity again.[5] Likewise, the promise of the kingdom, begun with the call of Abraham from the east, from Shinar, was fulfilled in a great company of his descendants possessing the land of Palestine with victory over enemies under David. But at last moral chaos filled the land (cf. the latter prophets), and the word of divine judgment was pronounced (cf. Isaiah 29, Jeremiah 1) that the kingdom was to be destroyed by enemies, the people taken captive to the east again, to Shinar (Jeremiah 52).[6]

Prophetic judgment is perhaps most clearly seen in its antithetical relationship to the creative word by a comparison of biblical cursing and blessing.[7] From the protological divine creation of man in Genesis (cf. Gen 1:28; 3:17) to the eschatological

---

[5] So much so that the true Heir of David was born in Bethlehem's stables in the company of shepherds (cf. Luke 2:8-20).

[6] This is precisely the statement implicit in the structure of Matt 1:17.

[7] Yet in his excellent study, *Grundformen Prophetischer Rede* (München: C. Kaiser, 1940), pp. 13-14, Claus Westermann noted that the concept of the

judgment of Christ in Matthew (cf. Matt 25:34, 41), blessing and cursing describe a duality of destiny fundamental to the whole of biblical understanding. The divine word in Gen 1:28 informs the essential concept of biblical blessing. In the creation account, man is charged with being fruitful upon the earth and ruling over it, and the divine blessing is furnished as man's empowerment to this duty. The essence, then, of biblical blessing is all that fosters man's fertility and assists him to achieve dominion: everything which promotes vitality[8] and victory.[9] Elohim is the one creating life, so opening or shutting the womb,[10] while El Elyon is the one dividing the nations, so deciding victory or defeat.[11] The creative blessing of God is foundational to the Abrahamic covenant wherein God blesses Sarah as the mother of the nations (fertility) and kings (dominion; cf. Gen 17:16), while this same blessing finds poetic continuance in the blessing of Rebekah that she should be the mother of myriads possessing the gate of their enemies (Gen 24:60). On the other hand, when disobedience to the divine word enters the biblical drama the consequence is the curse,[12] the essence of which is everything hindering fertility and resisting dominion: that which furthers death[13] and defeat.[14] Consequently, the curse of Cain removes the fertility of the ground (Gen 4:11-12), and the curse of Canaan brings servitude (Gen 9:25-27).

The power of the divine word of blessing or cursing and its

---

prophetic curse and blessing had not yet been accorded serious study. In a subsequent work on biblical blessing, Westermann registered his amazement that no major Old or New Testament theology assigns a distinctive significance to the concept of blessing in the whole range of divine dealings with man, an amazement which could justifiably have been shared with reference to biblical cursing as well (cf. *Blessing in the Bible and the Life of the Church*, trans. Keith Crim [Philadelphia: Fortress, 1978], p. 15). This neglect is yet more astonishing in view of recent archaeological testimony to the significance of blessing and cursing to the ancient Near Eastern covenantal framework.

[8] Cf. Exod 23:25-26; Deut 7:12-15; and J. Pedersen, *Israel*, 2 vols., trans. by Mrs. Aslaug Møller (London: Oxford University, 1926), vol. 1, pp. 182-212.

[9] Cf. Exod 23:27-28; Deut 7:16.

[10] Cf. the blessing of Jacob (Gen 49:25).

[11] Cf. the blessing of Melchizedek (Gen 14:20; also Deut 32:8; Ps 110:4-6).

[12] F. Büchsel, *Theological Dictionary of the New Testament*, Gerhard Kittel, trans. Geoffrey W. Bromiley (Grand Rapids: Eerdmans, 1964-76), vol. 1, p. 449.

[13] Cf. Deut 27:16 and Exod 21:17.

[14] Cf. Deut 28:45-48 and Deut 30:19. The sphere of cursing applies in this manner to Adam and Eve in their respective judgments. The earth now resists the dominion of man, and woman finds her fertility impeded.

contingency upon obedience was the perpetual illustration of
Gerizim and Ebal to Israel, the one mountain testifying to the
sphere of life, the other mountain witnessing to the sphere of
death. Everything encouraging the creative blessing of God was
the consequence of obedience (Deut 28:1-14) while everything
contrary to the creative blessing was the result of disobedience
(Deut 28:15-68). Prophetic pronouncements of blessing and
cursing establish an antithetical parallelism consistent with the
two ways of life and death fundamental to the biblical world
perception. The thought is quite Johannine in its coloring of
light and darkness, that which leads to life and that leading to
death. The law sets before Israel decisions of life and death, the
prophets announce salvation and judgment, the writings introduce wisdom and folly, and the apostles write of the spirit and
flesh. Sigmund Mowinckel suggested that the struggle between
life and death transpired within the temple cultus in Israel, a
conflict reducible in cognate cultures to an essential dualism.[15]

Nevertheless, from the light shining into darkness in the first
creation (John 1:5) to the perpetual light of the new creation
(Rev 21:25) and from the protological creation of life (Gen 1:27)
to the eschatological death of death (1 Cor 15:54) scripture consistently and hopefully awaits the vindication of good over evil, of
the blessing over the curse. Such a clear affirmation, in contrast to
other ancient cultures,[16] is theologically necessary in Israel due to
the consistent monotheism of the Bible. It is from one God that
prophetic words of good and evil come forth. "Who is there who
speaks and it comes to pass, unless the Lord has commanded it? Is
it not from the mouth of the Most High that both good and evil go
forth?" (Lam 3:37-38).[17] This one God displays his wisdom by
infallibly accomplishing good purposes out of the evil designs of
man (cf. Gen 50:20). God vindicates his one beneficient purpose
in prophetic pronouncements by appending a word of comfort

[15] S. Mowinckel, *Religion und Kultus* (Göttingen: Vandenhoeck & Ruprecht,
1953), p. 63. Life and death struggles were known in Egypt (Horus and Seth) and
Canaan (Baʿal and Mot), though the contests were confused in polytheistic myth.
Naturalistic theologies often express a dualism dependent upon diurnal and
seasonal cycles. In the monotheistic theology of scripture, God appoints day and
night, summer and winter (Gen 8:22).

[16] While Persia approached a true moral fatalism (Ormazd and Ahriman), the
Norse lands awaited the day of Ragnarok, the victory of evil over good, a true
moral pessimism.

[17] Cf. Isa 45:7, in context possibly a polemic against Persian Zoroastrianism.

(*Heil*) to a word of woe (*Unheil*), the ultimate irony of transforming cursing into blessing. The prophetic oracle in Gen
3:14-19 is a paradigm of this principle. God vindicates his wrath
in retribution, but he manifests his mercy in restoration. It is a
message announcing inevitable death to Adam; yet it is a message
from which he derives the comforting hope of life.[18]

Prophetic Salvation

The nature of the prophetic word transforming cursing into
blessing in Gen 3:14-19 is the subject of the second part of this
chapter. Hermann Gunkel noted that poetry was the oldest form
of prophetic speech in almost every ancient culture, a medium
expressly suited to the ecstatic passion of the prophet.[19] The
oracle of destiny in Gen 3:14-19 is the primal model for such
poetic invention, and it is in fact cast in poetic irony, poetic
(wherein much may be signified by little stated)[20] and ironic
(whereby what is stated may be exceeded by or contrary to what is
signified).[21] The oracle in Gen 3:14-19 expresses retributive irony
to the serpent, the woman, and the man. But it likewise expresses
restorative irony to the woman and the man, wherein the curse is
transformed into blessing. Each will be examined in turn.

Retributive irony is evident in the condemnation of the
serpent: the most crafty of creatures (Gen 3:1) becomes the most
accursed (Gen 3:14). By ironic extension the serpent's judgment
characterizes the justice distributed to Satan and his seed. Like the
King of Babel who would ascend to the numinous assembly of the
north but is brought to the assembly of the dead in Sheol (Isa
14:9-15), so Herod would arrogate to himself the glory of God,
but the worm is appointed for his destruction (Acts 12:20-23).

---

[18] Cf. the naming of Eve (Gen 3:20).

[19] H. Gunkel, *Die Propheten* (Göttingen: Vandenhoeck & Ruprecht, 1917),
p. 119.

[20] Cf. the German *Dichtung* ("poetry") from *dichten* ("to make thick, to
pack").

[21] Extra-biblical prophetic utterances (cf. especially the Delphic and Sibyl-
line oracles) were likewise fond of poetic (uniformly in hexameter) irony (cf. the
word to Croessus that he would destroy a great kingdom [Herodotus 1:91] and the
word to Athens about the safety of her wooden walls [Herodotus 8:36], cf. also
Thucydides 2:54). Indeed so clouded were these pagan pronouncements that they
aroused the skepticism of Plutarch ("De Pythia Oraculis," 25) and Cicero ("De
Divinatione," 2:54).

The word play in Gen 3:15, "you shall bruise him on the heel" but "he shall bruise you on the head" (an irony of degree) establishes the judicial principle that as Satan had meeted out, so in fatal measure it is returned to him again. Thus the pharaoh of Egypt hurls the sons of Israel into the river (Exod 1:22), but God hurls the pharaoh of Egypt into the sea (Exod 15:4). Likewise the Philistines make sport with Samson in the temple (Judg 16:30), the wicked prepare a pit for David (Ps 9:15-16), Hamon prepares a gallows for Mordecai (Esth 7:10), and Satan erects a cross for Christ (1 Cor 2:8). Retributive irony likewise characterizes the prophetic judgment upon the woman: by desiring to rule over her husband she finds herself in perpetual subservience to him,[22] an irony of contraries. There is retributive irony in the judgment upon the man as well: the dust that would be like God (cf. Gen 3:22) is turned into dust again, an irony of consequence.

But the woman and the man are subjects of grace as well as wrath, and the prophetic oracle contains a pronouncement as well of restorative irony. There had been demonic irony in that the woman whose life was derived from man should become to him the minister of death. But there is divine irony in the appointing of the woman to be the mother of all living (Gen 3:20). The promise is given of a seed to subdue the serpent (Gen 3:15), and by restorative irony God ordains that the weak will conquer the strong. The Son that would vanquish the serpent would have a maid for a mother (Gal 4:4), and woman, who had delivered man to sin, would deliver him a Savior. The one who cries in the cradle will subdue the principalities of darkness (Matt 4:1-11), and he who sucks the breast will defeat the power of death (cf. Gen 3:15, 20).[23] Only the wisdom of God could appoint death as the way to life (Gal 2:20), the ultimate irony of curse transformed into blessing (Gal 3:13-14).[24] It was by the death of the last Adam that the

[22] Cf. Gen 3:16 with 4:7, and U. Cassuto, *From Adam to Noah* (Jerusalem: Magnes, 1959), pp. 165-66.

[23] Cf. Psalm 8, where the shepherd boy who conquered Goliath had detected the divine design to vanquish the avenger through the son of man.

[24] Two sacraments are appointed in the governance of God for the church, both displaying the divine wisdom in restorative irony. The first Adam by eating had found death (Gen 3:6), the last Adam made eating the means of finding life (Matt 26:26). In baptism the church is buried in death that she might be raised to life (Rom 6:4). This principle of restorative irony becomes a major theme in the New Testament, extending to the oxymoronic character of the Christian life. The Christian is wise, and yet a fool. He is poor, yet rich; last, and yet first; servant to

serpent of old encountered death and the first Adam found life. The nails that pierced the feet of Christ would bruise the heel, but they would crush the head of the serpent (1 Cor 2:8). The last Adam wore the thorns of the first Adam, but by these wounds he was healing his people (Isa 53:5). Christ knew the nakedness of Adam, but by this shame he was clothing his people in righteousness (Gal 3:27). For the first Adam the tree of knowledge brought death. But the last Adam knew death upon the tree bringing life (1 Pet 2:24). Adam had made a grave of a garden, but Christ would make a garden of a grave (Luke 24:5).

Conclusion

With Abraham God expressly revealed himself as Lord of the blessing and the curse (Gen 12:3), and with Balaam he revealed his wisdom in transforming cursing into blessing (Num 23:11). Yet both of these aspects of God's sovereignty are seen in the first prophetic oracle in Gen 3:14-19. The law would lift up the serpent in the wilderness (Num 21:9), but grace even so would lift up the Son, that he who became a curse upon the tree of death might become a blessing and the tree of life (Gal 3:13-14). Christ in retributive irony took the crafty by craftiness (1 Cor 3:19), and in restorative irony led captivity captive (Eph 4:8).

The tracing of benediction and malediction to the one beneficient purpose of the one God is the ground of the believer's hope. In this denial of the ultimacy of evil the Christian is delivered from a Persian pessimism, the victory promise of Gen 3:15 speaking peace to dying sons of Adam. The sin which brings death is not co-eternal with the ontological Trinity. Its career had a beginning (Ezek 28:15) and will assuredly know an end (Rev 20:10). The bride of the last Adam, though presently corruptible, will ultimately experience the putting on of incorruption. She shall witness the swallowing up of death in victory, the realization of victory through the Lord Jesus Christ, the vindication of good over evil, and the issue of all things into the greater glory of the singularly sovereign God.

> I form the light, and create darkness: I make peace, and create calamity: I the Lord do all these things. — Isa 45:7

---

all, and yet greatest in the kingdom; dying, and yet finding life (cf. Rom 8:36, 37; 2 Cor 4:8-12; 6:8-10; Matt 5:3-12; Luke 6:27, 29; 1 Pet 3:9).

6 | The City of God and the Cities of Men

In his exhortation to perseverance the author of Hebrews cites the fathers of faith as examples of those sacrificing a temporal for an eternal hope (cf. 11:9-10, 13, 39-40), of men and women in faith looking forward to the promise of the heavenly city "whose architect and builder is God" (11:10).[1] While faithless men of all ages beginning with Cain have built temporal cities, the eternal city upon heavenly Mount Zion (11:13, 16; 12:22) has been the eschatological hope of the faithful in every age beginning with Abel. The foundational hope of all prophecy is "the restoration of all things" (Acts 3:21),[2] and the consummating expectation of faith is the return of Edenic bliss in the dwelling together of God and man in the holy city, the New Jerusalem (cf. Rev 21:2-4; 22:1-4). Eden to God's people has ever been the promise of protology. Edenic Zion will be the fulfillment of eschatology.

If the author of Hebrews assumes that beginning with Abel men of faith have believed in and looked for the heavenly city, then surely the Old Testament must contain explicit teaching about it. This discussion of the city of God begins with a consideration of the cosmographical correspondences between the Eden of Genesis 2-3 and the Zion of Revelation 21-22, highlighting the interconnecting eschatological redemption of the city throughout the law, prophets, psalms, and apostles. The chapter continues with a discussion of the Edenic cosmology of the temple of Solomon as a microcosmic type of the New Jerusalem, the eschatological hope of pilgrims of faith in every age. The discussion concludes with a sketch of the cities of men. Enoch, Babel, and Sodom will be profiled; these are the cities of

[1] H. Strathmann, *Theological Dictionary of the New Testament*, ed. Gerhard Kittel, trans. Geoffrey W. Bromiley (Grand Rapids: Eerdmans, 1964-76), vol. 6, p. 531.

[2] H. Gressmann, *Der Messias* (Göttingen: Vandenhoeck & Ruprecht, 1929), p. 183.

chaos highlighted in Genesis. An attempt will be made to demonstrate that from the beginning urbanism is but a studied counterfeit of the heavenly city.

The Cosmographical Correspondences Between Eden and Zion

The cosmography presupposed in Genesis 2-3 depicts Eden as containing the world mountain[3] from whose numinous summit descended the great river of paradise whose waters fructified the four corners of the earth (2:10-14).[4] Upon this mountain was the garden planted by God, watered by the great river and containing the tree of life (2:9). Within the hedges of the pleasant garden, which was oriented to the four points of the compass, eastward (2:8; 3:24), Adam and his bride[5] walked in community with God. Revelation 21-22 depicts a similar cosmography in a redeemed creation. The evangelist is carried away in the Spirit to a great mountain (21:10) from whose summit descends the river of life nourishing the tree of life (22:1-2). The four-square city, oriented eastward (21:13), constitutes the community of faith which, like a bride adorned for her husband (21:2), walks in fellowship with God. The cosmographical correspondences between Genesis 2-3 and Revelation 21-22 reduce primarily to the concepts of a city within a garden upon a mountain. These concepts alone were sufficient to the oriental mind to describe both the old heavens and earth (Gen 2:1) and the new (Rev 21:1), notions difficult for our occidental understanding to translate into our categories of Euclidian space and Aristotelian time.[6]

---

[3] Ezekiel's Tyrian lament describes Eden upon the heights of the holy mountain of God (28:13-14). His vision of the new Eden (cf. 47:12) describes a temple-city on a very high mountain (40:2). John's vision in Revelation likewise sees a restored Eden (22:2) upon a great and high mountain (21:10).

[4] Four in scripture is the number of the earth, e.g., the four rivers of Eden, the four winds of the earth (Zech 6:5), and the four corners of the earth (Rev 20:8).

[5] To the oriental mind the bride (with her promise of fertility) represented the community of the city. Consequently, Eve ("the mother of all living," Gen 3:20) became a type of Edenic Zion, the holy city represented as a bride in Rev 21:2. Similarly, the psalmist sees Zion as the mother of the sons of Jacob (87:5) and the apostle conceives of the heavenly Jerusalem as the mother of the sons of promise (Gal 4:26). Cf. the ancient concept in *metropolis* or "mother city" with the LXX of Psalm 86:5 (=87:5) of Μήτηρ Σιών.

[6] The eagerness of evangelical apologists to superimpose a credible science upon the Bible often leads to a misunderstanding of the representational aspect of biblical imagery. To speak of heaven as a great home (John 14:2) with windows

Nevertheless, the Edenic city upon the cosmic mountain fully expresses the great redemptive hope of biblical eschatology throughout the testaments. These three cosmic themes of the mountain (as the inviolable cosmic foundation or "axis mundi"), the garden (as the source of all life-giving streams or "umbilicus mundi"), and the city (as the cosmopolitan community or "centrum mundi") will be traced in turn through the scripture to demonstrate their eschatological restoration.

The restoration of the Edenic mountain in scripture is to be identified with the eschatological exaltation of Zion as the cosmic mountain of the north. The conception of the earth in scripture is consistently after the pattern of heaven.[7] By analogy to the one fixed point of heaven (the cosmic cynosure or north star) the earth likewise contains a cosmic center (the mountain of the north or "Zaphon").[8] As the polar star alone is immovable within the encircling zodiac, so the eschatological Mount Zion is immovable within the encompassing mountains (Ps 125:1-2).[9] The resulting security of cosmic Zion from all chaos powers, whether natural or historic, is poetically portrayed in the psalms which Gunkel designated the Zion hymns. Psalm 46, for example, expresses the confidence that though the mountains slide into the sea and the waters of chaos assail, the Most High (Elyon) dwelling in the midst of Zion makes her mountain immovable and secure (Zion as "axis mundi," Pss 46:2-5; 125:1). Psalm 48 likewise portrays the kings of chaos[10] sailing the ships of Tarshish[11] against the

---

(Gen 8:2) or of earth as having four corners (Rev 20:8) and supporting the pillars of heaven (Job 26:11) is metaphoric or phenomenological in character, certainly not scientific. To read scripture with categories of current physical cosmology is to be robbed of the richness of heaven described under the figure of a home with God (John 14:2) or to lose the significance of hell described as a place of fire (Rev 20:15) and yet darkness (Jude 13).

[7] Cf. Heb 8:1-5 and the cosmic tabernacle; and also M. Kline, *Images of the Spirit* (Grand Rapids: Baker, 1980), p. 35ff.; B. Childs, *Myth and Reality in the Old Testament* (Naperville, Ill.: Allenson, 1960), p. 85.

[8] The "Zaphon" theology is identifiable in the law (Exod 15:17 cf. 14:2), the prophets (Isa 14:13), and Ps 48:2, where Zion is identified as the mountain of Zaphon.

[9] If Zion is immovable then it is eternal, according to the ancient conception of time (cf. Heb 12:25-29 and Aristotle's definition of time in *Physica* iv 11).

[10] Cf. Pss 2:1-6; 46:6-10; 48:4-7; 76:2-12; Ezek 39:9-10, and Rev 20:8-9.

[11] That is, from "Oceanus," the chaos waters. Tarshish was in the remotest known regions of the west, the place of sunset darkness (cf. Ps 139:9).

cosmic mountain. But Zion is fortified with towers and ramparts,[12] and the chaos kings are discomfited by fear,[13] their
weapons burned.[14] The prophetic literature anticipates the restoration of the cosmic mountain in the eschaton as Zion, topo-
graphically inferior to Olives, is ultimately exalted over Olives[15]
as the chief mountain of Israel (Isa 2:2-4 = Mic 4:1-3; Zech 14:4-
10), from whose heights the evangelist will herald renewed Edenic
peace to the earth.[16]

The restoration of Eden upon Mount Zion was the hope
foreseen by Isaiah, "Indeed the LORD will comfort Zion; he will
comfort all her waste places. And her wilderness he will make like
Eden, and her desert like the garden of the LORD" (51:3). In the
eschaton, the river of paradise will issue forth from Zion, once
again becoming a fountain of life nourishing the earth ("umbilicus mundi" Ps 36:8-9, cf. the LXX of Judg 9:37; Ezek 38:12,
ὀμφαλὸς τῆς γῆς of Zion).[17] Springs of living water will issue
from the throne of the living God (Ps 36:8; Jer 17:13; Ezek 47:1;
Rev 22:1), forming a great river which for abundance can fill the
seas (Zech 14:8), for charm will delight the city of God (Ps 46:4),
for beauty will be clear as crystal (Rev 22:1), for efficacy can make
the salty sweet (Ezek 47:8-9), for cleansing will wash iniquity
from the inhabitants of Jerusalem (Zech 13:1), and for healing
will give drink to the tree of life (Ezek 47:12; Rev 22:2). The
removal of the Edenic curse (Zech 14:11; Rev 22:3) will so trans-
form nature that even the desert will blossom with beauty (Isaiah
35), filling the earth with grain and fruit (Isa 4:2; Amos 9:13), and

[12] The circuit procession suggested in Ps 48:12 is to be contrasted with the
Israelite experience at Jericho. While God collapses the walls of the cities of chaos,
Zion's foundations are firm. Ultimately the eschatological security of Zion is
expressed figuratively by her ever-open gates (Ezek 38:11; Rev 21:25).

[13] The overthrow of the chaos kings is expressed through the greatest fear of
man (flight before an enemy, Ps 48:5) and the greatest fear of woman (anguish of
childbirth, Ps 48:6), expressions constituting a merism indicating total and final
destruction.

[14] Destruction with the fire of God is a common motif for those assailing the
cosmic mountain (cf. Pss 46:9; 76:3; Ezek 39:9-10; Rev 20:9).

[15] The Olivet Ridge east of Zion was the site of Solomon's abominations
(2 Kgs 23:13). The eschatological exaltation of Zion likewise includes the humiliation of Olives (Zech 14:4, cf. also Acts 1:11-12 and Matt 24:3).

[16] From the high mountain of eschatological Zion the Isaianic evangelist
cries out the good news of the rule of God (Isa 40:9; cf. 52:7; Rom 10:15 and
especially Ps 72:3, 16).

[17] R. Clifford, *The Cosmic Mountain in Canaan and the Old Testament*
(Cambridge: Harvard University, 1972), pp. 135, 183.

making of Israel a land flowing with milk and honey, oil and wine (cf. Isa 27:2-6; Hos 2:22; Joel 3:18; Amos 9:13). The restoration of Edenic peace in the animal kingdom,[18] foreshadowed in Israel by the law (Lev 26:6), is realized in the eschaton of the prophets as a result of the covenant of peace (Ezek 34:26; cf. Isa 11:6-9; 35:4). Likewise Edenic peace will prevail again in the community of men as the nations hammer swords into plowshares and spears into pruning hooks (Isa 2:4; cf. Mic 5:10-11; Zech 9:10; Pss 46:10; 76:4).

The restoration of Edenic community—peace between God and man—finds its highest realization in the New Jerusalem[19] of Rev 21:2. The holy city, like Eve, adorned in bridal innocence and made ready for the Son of Man (Rev 21:9), symbolizes the perfected goodness of paradise, containing the river and the tree of life (Rev 22:2). The four-square dimensions of the city upon the mountain[20] are reminiscent of the cuboidal form of the Mosaic inter-sanctum, representing the cosmic coextensiveness of the holy of holies with the new heavens and earth as redeemed men tabernacle together with God (Rev 21:3).[21] Because there is nothing that defiles, there is no temple (Rev 21:22); nevertheless, in the New Jerusalem there is Christ, who is the true Shekinah (Rev 21:22; cf. John 2:21), and there are his people, who constitute the true santuary (Rev 3:12). The prophetic vision of the Old Testament had likewise foreseen God laying the foundations of Edenic Zion upon the holy mountain (Ps 87:1-2; Ezek 40:2), a refuge city (Isa 57:13) for God's chosen ones (Isa 65:9) which, like Eden, is remote and removed from all uncleanness (Isa 52:1; Joel 3:17; Obad 17). The eschatological evangel proclaimed by Isaiah has the nations represented in Zion under the figure of animals and trees consistent with the Edenic character of exalted Zion. Camels from Midian, flocks from Kedar, rams from Nebaioth will come to glorify the house of God (Isa 60:6-7). Likewise, the cedar of

---

[18] Gressmann derived the understanding of peace among the animals of Eden from the absence of the carnivore (Gen 1:29), *Der Messias*, p. 152, cf. also Gen 2:19.

[19] In scripture the eschatological "new" carries a redemptive nuance, cf. the new song, new creation, new covenant, new man, new heavens and earth.

[20] The conceptual combination of a square with a mountain describes a pyramid, a physical structure so widespread in antiquity.

[21] Cf. M. Woudstra, "The Tabernacle in Biblical-Theological Perspective," *New Perspectives on the Old Testament*, ed. J. Barton Payne (Waco, Texas: Word, 1970), pp. 100-101.

Lebanon, the juniper, the box tree, and the cypress[22] beautify in ecumenical richness the city of the Lord and the place of his sanctuary (Isa 60:13-14). In his very instructive work entitled *The Meaning of the City,* Jacques Ellul observed that the prophetic literature is filled with the expectation of God building an Edenic temple-city upon a great mountain.[23] This sanctuary-city, founded and built by God alone (Exod 15:17; Pss 78:68-69; 87:1-2; Heb 11:10; Rev 21:2), is to become the joy of the whole earth ("centrum mundi," cf. Ps 48:2; Isa 62:7) and the herald of peace will resound from the heights of the exalted city, summoning the nations to come to the city of peace (Pss 2:10-12; 46:8-11; Isa 60:14) bringing tribute (Isa 60:6-9; Pss 68:18; 72:10; Hag 2:7), petitioning the favor of the Great King (Isa 2:1-3; Ps 2:10-12; Zech 8:20-23), and learning his law (Isa 2:1-3; 11:9).

Zion's Temple, a Cosmological Type of Paradise

The cosmology of the Old Testament is fond of describing creation as a tabernacle which God has pitched (cf. Psalm 104; Job 9:8; Isa 40:22) or a house which God has established (with pillars, windows, and doors; Job 26:11; Gen 7:11; Ps 78:23).[24] Consequently, the temple of Zion, as a sanctuary which God has established, becomes a microcosmic metaphor for creation itself. This idea finds explicit expression in Ps 78:69: "And he built his sanctuary like the heights, like the earth which he has founded forever."[25]

In the New Testament this same idea finds implicit expression in Matthean theology. The disciples understand Christ's prophecy of the destruction of the temple as signifying the end of the cosmos (Matt 24:1-39), and the rending of the temple veil (cf. Heb 10:20) brings about the rending of the earth (Matt 27:51).[26]

---

[22] The supernatural character of Edenic Zion is indicated by the presence together of trees which never occur elsewhere together in nature.

[23] J. Ellul, *The Meaning of the City,* trans. Dennis Pardee (Grand Rapids: Eerdmans, 1970), pp. 189ff.

[24] Cf. W. Eichrodt, *Theologie des Alten Testaments,* 2 vols. (Leipzig: J. C. Hinrichs, 1935), vol. 2, pp. 45-46; and E. Jacob, *Theology of the Old Testament,* trans. A. Heathcote and P. Allcock (New York: Harper and Row, 1958), pp. 144-49.

[25] Cf. Ps 150:1 and O. Keel, *The Symbolism of the Biblical World,* trans. T. Hallett (New York: Seabury, 1978), p. 175.

[26] Cf. a possible juxtaposition of the temple-cosmos parallel in Pauline

Since the temple of Zion represented the cosmic house of creation to the Israelite, we may assume that the cosmological correspondences between the temple (microcosm) and creation (macrocosm) would largely reduce to the concepts of the mountain, the garden, and the city. Once again, with reference to Solomon's temple, these notions will be examined in turn.

The idea of the cosmic mountain, with reference to the Solomonic temple, is associated with the highground of Zion foundationally, and with the bronze pillars (Jachin and Boaz) symbolically. In the Song of the Sea, which contains the earliest scriptural reference to the sanctuary, Moses remarks that God would establish the place of his dwelling upon the mountain of his inheritance (Exod 15:17; cf. Ps 78:54), a passage alluded to by Solomon in his dedicatory prayer for the temple.[27] Consequently, Solomon's temple was built upon the highground of Mount Zion, the acropolis of ancient Jerusalem.[28] Consistent with this thought, the pilgrims of faith poetically go up to Zion (עָלָה, Ps 122:4) to worship the Most High God (עֶלְיוֹן, Ps 46:4) who dwells there.[29] In his eighth night vision, the prophet Zechariah describes four winds of heaven coming forth from the presence of God, who dwells behind two bronze mountains.[30] The mountains, in the metaphor of a house, become pillars, and the two

---

theology in 2 Thess 2:4, 8. The man of sin in the temple of God brings about the cosmic day of wrath.

[27] The expression מָכוֹן לְשִׁבְתְּךָ from Exod 15:17 is directly applied by Solomon to Zion at the temple dedication (1 Kgs 8:13 = 2 Chr 6:2).

[28] The relative prominence of the temple precincts is suggested by the designation of the site as Moriah (cf. Gen 22:2–3, cf. also the LXX τὴν γῆν τὴν ὑψηλὴν) and by its serviceability as a threshing floor (2 Chr 3:1). However, the true significance is not topographical but spiritual. Ezekiel's vision describes a temple-city upon a very high mountain (Ezek 40:2), while John, in the Spirit, sees the New Jerusalem likewise upon a very high mountain (Rev 21:10).

[29] The conviction that deity dwells upon a mountain (and by way of contrast, the wicked dwell in the abyss, cf. Luke 8:31; Rev 9:1) is pervasive in antiquity. For the Syrians, god dwelt upon Mt. Casios; for the Greeks, the divine residence was upon Mt. Olympus. The Hindus regarded Mt. Meru as a divine residence. The Mesopotamians (like the Egyptians) lacked natural mountains and so built the *zigguratu* (Assyrian-Babylonian "mountain-top"), a tower or step-pyramid surmounted by a temple. Each step-like stage had a different color of brick, a structure presenting a picture strikingly parallel to John's vision of the heavenly Zion (cf. Rev 21:19–20; Isa 54:11–12). Cf. also the staged pyramids throughout Meso-America.

[30] Zech 6:1–5. The four winds come forth like the four rivers of paradise. The garden itself was oriented to the east, that is, to the four points of the compass.

free-standing bronze pillars (Jachin and Boaz) set at the entrance
to Solomon's temple were identified by Gressmann as representing these cosmic mountains, which in ancient cosmography
supported the weight of the heavens.[31] Similar pillars were noted
by Herodotus before the temple of Melqart in Tyre,[32] a Phoeni-
cian divinity the Greek historian identified with Hercules, after
whom the straights of Gibraltar (the pillars of Hercules) were
named. In classical mythology these mountains became the cosmic focal point of the heavens resting upon the earth.[33] Similarly,
the biblical model for Hercules, Samson, is associated with the
pillars of the Philistine temple of Gaza upon which the weight of
the temple was supported.[34] Finally, the capitals of the Solomonic
pillars displayed pomegranates, a fertility emblem,[35] suggesting
the garden at the summit of the mountain, once again clearly a
paradise motif.[36]

[31] Cf. Gressmann, *Der Messias*, pp. 170-71. This opinion has been challenged. W. Kornfeld ("Der Symbolismus der Templesäulen," *ZAW* 74 [1962],
pp. 50-57) follows Albright in identifying the bronze pillars with the Osirian
Djed column. A more satisfying suggestion might be to relate the pillars to the
gate entrance to Egyptian temples the Greeks called the *pylon*, twin truncated
mountains between which the winged Aten of Egyptian iconography symbolized
the sunrise. Cf. also the *propylaea* gate of the Athenian acropolis.

[32] Herodotus, *The History*, ii, 44. This is significant due to the influence of
Tyrian craftsmen upon Solomon's builders (cf. 1 Kings 5).

[33] This is recounted in the Atlas story. Interestingly, Atlas was the father of
the Hesperides, who guarded the pleasant garden beyond the pillars of Hercules,
from whom the Greek hero was seeking the golden apples.

[34] The pillars of the Dagon temple, though incorporated into the temple
structure itself, represented the same notion as the free standing columns of
Solomon's temple, namely, that they supported the weight of the cosmos. It is
interesting to speculate regarding the cosmic significance of the blinded Samson
(from שֶׁמֶשׁ, Hebrew for sun) standing between the two pillars prior to the
destruction of the temple. Note also the darkened left eye (lunar disc) of Horus in
the astral course of the Aten between the pylon mountains. Cf. further the solar
darkness at the death of Christ, the true Temple (Matt 27:45). Sidereal eclipse is
consistently a sign of cosmic overthrow (cf. Isa 13:10; Ezek 32:7; Mark 13:24-25;
Acts 2:19-20).

[35] Cf. Cant 4:3; 6:7, 11; 7:12; 8:2 and O. Keel, *Symbolism*, p. 164.

[36] Two paradise motifs popular in the architecture of antiquity were the
notions of the word of god and the fertility it created. Representations of these
ideas are seen in the Greek columnar architecture of Corinth, the column capital
displaying the acanthus leaf (cf. the Egyptian lotus capital) for fertility, and in the
Ionic column, the capital portraying a scroll (cf. the Egyptian papyrus capital)
representing the word of god telling of life and death (the egg and dart pattern). It
is instructive to note also the prominence of the high places in Canaanite idolatry
(cf. 1 Kgs 14:23; Exod 34:12-13; Deut 12:2; 16:21), the אֲשֵׁרָה often represented as
trees planted on the mountain top and representing fertility.

The holy of holies of Solomon's temple appears to have been a very conscious symbolic reconstruction of the garden of Eden. The room itself was a perfect square,[37] oriented like Eden to the eastern sunrise.[38] Just as the cherubim had barred Adam's access to the garden of God (Gen 3:24),[39] so they guarded the temple throne of God. On the outside of the holy of holies, the cherubim guarded access through their representations woven into the veil.[40] On the inside the cherubim were represented by gilded wooden figures whose wings spanned, and thus protected, the entire room. Solomon constructed the room itself with wood from the cedar, cypress, olive, and palm trees in gold inlay.[41] The acacia and almond were also there, along with figures of flowers and palm trees. Lions were represented, and the swallow made her nest there.[42] It was a place of song[43] and the nearness of God (Ps 73:28). The ark of the testimony[44] gave the name oraculum (cf. דְּבִיר, from דָּבַר?) to the place where Israel, like Adam, heard the voice of God (Gen 3:8; cf. Exod 25:21–22; Num 7:89).

[37] In the eschaton the New Jerusalem becomes coextensive with the holy of holies, the sacred city assuming the cuboidal dimensions of the ancient inter-sanctum (that is, equal length, breadth, and height; cf. Rev 21:16). Cf. Woudstra, *New Perspectives*, pp. 100–101.

[38] The east is often identified as the place of salvation (cf. Ps 46:5; Mark 16:2). God always approaches his temple from the east (cf. Ezek 43:2; Zech 14:4). Interestingly, the first advent of Christ is announced by the star of the east (Matt 2:2), while the second advent is announced by lightning from the east (Matt 24:27).

[39] The emplacement of guardian figures to protect holy precincts from those who would defile is pervasive in the iconography of the ancient orient. Composite sphinx-like figures guarded the entrance to Assyrian palaces (called *kuribū*, cf. Keel, *Symbolism*, p. 123). The avenue of Amon sphinxes guarded the entrance to Karnak in the Egyptian Thebes. In Greek literature a sphinx likewise guarded the Thebes of Thessaly.

[40] The beginning of the eschaton is represented in the New Testament by the removal of the temple veil upon the death of the last Adam (Matt 27:51), signifying the open entry once again to paradise (Luke 23:43; Rev 2:7).

[41] The gold inlay reminds one of the precious stones in golden settings decorating the breastplate of the priest, perhaps a paradise motif (cf. Gen 2:12; Isa 54:11–12; Ezek 28:13; Rev 21:19–20 and 1 Cor 3:12–17).

[42] Lions (1 Kgs 7:36) and swallows (Ps 84:3) were associated with the holy place. Cf. the eschatological Edenic imagery of Isa 60:6–8.

[43] The temple was the place of musical instruments and choirs. That music is also a paradise motif is suggested by Ezek 28:13 (tamborines, cf. AV) and possibly Job 38:4–7. If the technology of the Cainite line was directed toward a reconstruction of paradise, as will be argued, then Jubal as the father of those playing lyre and pipe (Gen 4:21) is significant.

[44] The ark of the covenant as the throne of God becomes the source of the river of paradise in the eschaton (Ezek 47:1; Rev 22:1; cf. also the association of the

The temple of Zion was not simply the dwelling place of God; it was the place where God dwelt among men (cf. John 1:14).[45] This restoration of Edenic community, the tabernacling[46] together of God and man in the holy city,[47] was represented in ritual during the festival of booths.[48] This idea of the holy city, expressed by the Solomonic temple during Succoth, had been first represented by the tabernacle, the prototype of the temple, in the amphictyonic encampment[49] in the wilderness. It would be finally represented by the church, the antitype of the temple, as God would erect a spiritual edifice built of living stones.[50]

The Cities of Men: Parodies of Paradise

The author of Hebrews teaches that beginning with Abel men of faith have had their hope in heaven, not in earth (Heb 11:13-16), that they, like Abraham, have been called out from the

---

Gihon spring of Jerusalem with the Gihon river of paradise). It is interesting to speculate regarding the appropriateness of the articles within the ark to the theme of paradise. The ark contained the manna, Aaron's rod, and the tables of the law (Heb 9:4). The manna of the wilderness, bread given by God without the labor of man (Exod 16:32), was in color like bdellium (cf. Gen 2:12; Num 11:7). The rod of Aaron had subdued the kingdom of the serpent (cf. Gen 3:15; Exod 7:9-12). The law of life and death was the subject of the commandments (cf. Gen 2:16-17; Deut 30:19-20).

[45] This idea finds beautiful expression in Johannine theology (cf. John 14:1-3; Rev 21:3).

[46] The tabernacle (mobile) and the temple (immobile) are conceptually combined in Ps 27:4-6 as the place of protection for the psalmist, where he dwells in joy with the Lord.

[47] That the temple became the model for the cosmic city is evident in Ezekiel. Though describing the dimensions of a temple (Ezekiel 40-48), the prophet sees a structure like a city set upon a very high mountain (Ezek 40:2; cf. Rev 21:10).

[48] The faithful pilgrims of Israel in festival would go up to the temple of Zion singing the ascent psalms. Typically, they represented the faithful of all nations, that is, true Israel, who in the eschaton would stream to Zion to dwell in the cosmic city upon the mountain (cf. Pss 72:9-11; 117:1; 138:4; Hag 2:7-9; Zech 2:10-11; and cf. especially the Isaianic Apocalypse in 60:3-20 with Rev 21:1-27).

[49] The twelve tribes were arranged around the tabernacle three to a side, in quadrilateral *campus* formation. Oriented to the four points of the compass, the Israelite encampment would be similar to the four-square city of Rev 21:16, where God tabernacled with man (cf. Rev 21:3). The tabernacle and the city of Zion become coextensive in Isa 4:5-6, the fundamental passage, from which Rev 21:3 most likely derived.

[50] John the Baptist magnified God's power that of stones he could raise up sons to Abraham. But the Apostle Peter magnified God's mercy that of true sons of Abraham, God could raise up living stones in the temple of God (cf. Luke 3:8; 1 Pet 2:5 and Eph 2:21-22; 1 Cor 3:10-16; 1 Tim 3:15).

earthly Ur to tabernacle as strangers seeking the heavenly Salem. Beginning with Cain, however, faithless men have put their hope in earth, erecting visible cities. Consequently, it is the pattern for the wicked to be the city builders, not the righteous.[51] These cities of man portrayed in Genesis are but parodies of the true paradise. Like Babel they may have their "inviolable" tower whose top reaches into heaven (Gen 11:4), like Sodom they may have the appearance of the "garden of the LORD," (Gen 13:10), and like Enoch they may boast of a community (Gen 4:17), but they represent the work of man, not God (contrast the heavenly Zion, Heb 11:10), so they are ultimately cities of destruction. This chapter will conclude with a brief consideration of the cities of chaos highlighted in Genesis: the antediluvian Enoch and postdiluvian Babel and Sodom.

The founder of the great city of Enoch ("dedication," "founding"?) was Cain. Unlike Abel, who looked for the heavenly paradise of the city whose architect and builder is God (Heb 11:10), Cain set out to found and build an earthly city, his descendants developing a technology suited to creating an earthly paradise.[52] Cain's city was located in the east (Gen 4:16), which would have been watered by the Tigris, the easternmost river of paradise (Gen 2:14). Founded by a fratricide[53] who lived in fear of his life,[54] the city through its community would have afforded a place of security. This city of the Cainite line was apparently unrivaled as the great cosmopolis of antiquity. Through intermarriage (Gen 6:2) its citizens subdued the earth to the apostasy of their father Cain, filling the world with violence. Such was the ruin of sin

---

[51] Only in bondage does Israel build treasure cities (מִסְכְּנוֹת) for pharaoh (Exod 1:11) and Solomon (2 Chr 8:4-6).

[52] The τέχνη of Cain's descendants is remarkable in its similarity to the skills required to erect the tabernacle in the wilderness. In Jabal they have their tents, but no tent of meeting. In Jubal they have their pipes, but no psalms to sing. In Tubal-cain they have their craftsman, but no tabernacle to furnish. Such is the nature of urban man. (Cf. the τέχνη of Babylon, Rev 18:22.)

[53] Augustine takes note that Cain murdered his brother Abel, so also Romulus killed Remus, that the city might carry his name (*The City of God*, xv 5). The identification of Rome as the chaotic earthly city is perhaps suggested also in its sitting upon seven hills, a city like Babylon (Rev 17:9). The idea that the heavenly city had seven mountains is an ancient one, implicitly suggested in Prov 9:1 (wisdom's house of creation rests on seven pillars) and explicitly noted in 1 Enoch 32. The chaos cities have in common the sacking of Jerusalem; Babylon destroys the first temple and Rome the second.

[54] Cf. Plato on the origin of the *polis* (*Protagoras* 322-23).

wrought upon God's creative mandate to subdue and fill the earth by this archetypical city of chaos. The flood of Noah was the overthrow of this first great urban enterprise of fallen man.

Postdiluvian Genesis records the history of Babel and Sodom, two cities of man which become spiritual types of the earthly city (cf. 1 Pet 3:13; Rev 11:8). Like Enoch, Babel was founded in the east (Gen 11:2). It was watered by the Euphrates, one of the rivers of paradise (Ps 137:1).[55] Babel represented the rebellion of man against the divine command to subdue the earth under God, for the spirit of Babel was federal and imperial to the glory of man (Gen 11:4) and the state (Gen 10:10). Founded as a garden city upon a plain (Gen 11:2), Babel nevertheless lacked the mountain motif of paradise, but by technology its citizens set about to build a tower which would reach into heaven. In the judgment of God upon this earthly city the unfinished tower (Gen 11:8) remained as a remembrance of the frustrated purposes of man to subdue the earth in disobedience. Like Enoch and Babel, Sodom is associated in scripture with the east (Gen 13:11). It was watered by the Jordan, giving every outward appearance of the garden of paradise (Gen 13:10). Sodom, however, represented the rebellion of man against the divine mandate to be fruitful and multiply, and the sin of Sodom, to which the city gave its name (Deut 23:17), represented the rejection of God as Creator and the exchange of the truth for a lie (Rom 1:25). Founded as a garden city upon a plain (Gen 13:10), Sodom likewise lacked the mountain motif of paradise, but the judgment of God upon this earthly city left the pillar of salt,[56] a mocking reminder that the spirit of this city was contrary to the fertility associated with the mountain of the true paradise.

These cities of men often have the appearance of paradise, but never the reality. Like Cain in his sacrifice they may present a form of godliness, but they deny its power. By building high towers and ramparts to surround themselves, the earthly city dwellers seek safety from man and not God. By planting gardens to beautify their cities, the wicked would enjoy the aesthetic without the ethic; by collectivizing themselves the disobedient

---

[55] Herodotus celebrated the fertility of Babylon (*History* i, 193). Babylon would later be known for its hanging gardens and its temple-tower, *Etemenanki*, the "meeting place of heaven and earth."

[56] Salt symbolizes Sodom's infertility (Zeph 2:9; cf. Judg 9:45; Jer 17:6).

seek a community without a covenant. Such is the character of Babylon the Great. The heavenly Zion, however, is promised to those who would inherit the city of God by faith (Heb 11:39-40; 12:22-24). The heavenly city is a mountain secure from all who would spiritually defile (Rev 21:27, 22:15), its outward garden-like beauty reflecting a spiritual comeliness (Rev 21:2) and its citizens constituting a covenant city sharing a spiritual re-birth (Heb 12:23; Rev 22:14). Such is the character of the New Jerusalem.

7 | The Flood of Noah and Prophetic Judgment

The great monotheistic affirmation of scripture requires the doctrine of catastrophic judgment to reconcile the holy wrath of heaven with the unrighteousness of earth. Moreover, the similarities between the great judgments recorded in scripture demonstrate the unity of prophetic pronouncement and the consistency of God's moral governance of world history. This chapter proposes first to demonstrate that the flood of Noah establishes the fundamental paradigm of biblical judgment recurring in the destructions of Sodom, Egypt, Canaan, Jerusalem (both the first and second temples), and the present cosmos.[1] This pattern of judgment is reducible to three elements: the "days of Noah," the "flood" of judgment, and the deliverance of the remnant from wrath. Second, this chapter proposes to demonstrate that the catastrophic judgments, modeled after the flood narrative of Genesis 6–7, are with respect to Jerusalem preceded by historical records synthetically parallel to Genesis 1–5.

The Judgment of Sodom

The destruction of the wicked city of Sodom is compared in the New Testament with the judgment of the flood. Christ establishes an equivalence between the days of Noah and the days of Lot, both of which are compared to the days of the Son of Man (Luke 17:26–30). Likewise, Peter compares the judgment of the ancient world and the deliverance of Noah with the destruction of Sodom and Gomorrah and the deliverance of Lot (2 Pet 2:5–8). The cities of the plain are overthrown by the fire of God metaphorically described as rain from heaven (מָטַר, Gen 19:24; 7:4).[2]

---

[1] While flood parallels are primary in the characterization of these judgments, there is a stereoscopic use of symbolism whereby the later prophets may appeal to previous catastrophic judgments for secondary comparisons.

[2] Cf. the record of Gibeah of Benjamin (Judg 19:22–20:40). The notion that Israel has become like Sodom and consequently stands in the way of catastrophic

63

While the wicked are utterly destroyed (שָׁחַת, Gen 19:13; 6:17),
Lot, like Noah, finds grace in the eyes of God (Gen 19:19; 6:8) to
the deliverance of his house (Gen 19:12; 7:7). The door of Lot's
house, like the door of the ark, is shut by heaven (Gen 19:10; 7:16),
consigning the wicked of earth to judgment, while Lot's household finds safety in the mountains (Gen 19:17, 30; 8:4).[3]

The Judgment of Egypt

The destruction of Egypt is wrought by Moses, artfully presented in the Pentateuch as the new Noah.[4] Like Noah, Moses'
life was delivered from the waters by an ark (תֵּבָה is unique to
Noah and Moses: Exod 2:3; Gen 6:14) daubed with pitch. As
Noah's household was baptized by the flood (1 Pet 3:20–21), so
Israel was baptized by the sea (1 Cor 10:2), God bringing the dry
land out of the deep for his people (חָרְבָה/חָרֵב, Exod 14:21; Gen
8:13), while destroying the enemies of godliness with the mighty
waters (Exod 15:10; Gen 7:19). While the Egyptians had suffered
the wrath of heaven, the faithful in Israel had found safety behind
the door of the Passover (Exod 12:21–23; Gen 7:16), and with
their flocks and herds they were delivered through the deep
(Exod 14:38; Gen 7:13–14) to be brought by God through forty
years of testing to find rest in the mountain of his inheritance
(Exod 15:17; Gen 8:4).

The Judgment of Canaan

The comparability of the days of Joshua[5] to the days of Noah
is established in the Pentateuch by the reference to the giants in
the land (נְפִילִים is unique to Num 13:33 and Gen 6:4). Moreover,
the language of the eisodus is marked by references analogous to
the flood narrative: (1) the Jordan was in flood like the sea

---

judgment is proclaimed by Isaiah (1:10), Jeremiah (23:14; Lam 4:6), Ezekiel
(16:46), Hosea (11:8), Amos (4:11), and Christ (Matt 11:23–24).

    [3] Cf. the Noahic pattern of Lot's sin: (1) he was drunk with the fruit of the
vine, (2) he became shamefully naked, (3) he knew not when he was uncovered,
and (4) he became father to the seed of strife, Moab and Ammon (Gen 19:30–38;
9:19–25).

    [4] U. Cassuto, *A Commentary on the Book of Exodus*, trans. Israel Abrahams
(Jerusalem: Magnes, 1967), pp. 18–19.

    [5] Joshua is presented as a new Moses (Josh 1:5; 3:7; 5:15).

(Josh 3:16; Exod 15:8), (2) the waters of the flood dried up when the soles of the feet of the priests carrying the ark found rest (Josh 3:13: כְּנוֹחַ כַּפּוֹת רַגְלֵי; Gen 8:9: מָנוֹחַ לְכַף־רַגְלָהּ), (3) the house of Israel passed over to dry land (חָרַב/חָרָבָה, Josh 4:18; Gen 8:13) while the waters returned to their place. The correlative to the flood in the judgment of Canaan was the ban (חֵרֶם/חָרַם, Deut 20:17; Josh 6:21; Gen 7:22-23) by which everything having the breath of life was to be destroyed by the sword. Although the Canaanites of Jericho were utterly destroyed, righteous Rahab[6] delivered her father's household (Josh 2:19; Gen 7:16), like Noah finding safety behind the door (Josh 2:19). Like Lot, Rahab was delivered from the city before it was burned on its tell (Josh 6:23-24).

The Judgment of Jerusalem
(First Temple)

The armies of Assyria that assailed Judah were compared by Isaiah to a great flood of waters (Isa 8:7-8; 17:12-13, cf. Amos 8:8; 9:5). The Chaldeans who conquered Jerusalem would be compared to the waters of Noah (cf. Isa 54:9: כִּי־מֵי נֹחַ זֹאת לִי).[7] The destruction of Jerusalem is comparable also to the judgment of Sodom (Isa 1:9; Lam 4:6), while Jeremiah used the language of chaos to color this destruction (Jer 4:23-26). The flood of judgment coming upon Jerusalem is described as wrath poured out of the windows of heaven (כִּי־אֲרֻבּוֹת מִמָּרוֹם נִפְתָּחוּ, Isa 24:18, cf. Gen 7:11; 8:2),[8] overturning the entire cosmic order (Isa 24:19). Wrath is poured out upon Zion as a consuming fire (Lam 4:11; cf. 2 Chr 36:19), as with Sodom's overthrow (cf. Deut 29:21-23). The covenant faithfulness of God that spared a remnant through the flood of Noah will likewise preserve a faithful remnant of Israel (Isa 54:9-11). The righteous are called upon to return to their chambers to seek shelter behind the door of safety (Isa 26:20; cf. Exod 12:21-23 and Gen 7:16) until the Lord brings the remnant

---

[6] Consider the mercy of God to the house of this woman! Righteous Rahab was a Canaanite harlot (cf. Gen 9:25) bearing the name of the anti-creative serpent.

[7] The deliverance of a remnant in Israel, as in the ark of Noah, is suggested by this simile in Isaiah's Book of Consolation.

[8] Jack P. Lewis, *A Study of the Interpretation of Noah and the Flood in Jewish and Christian Literature* (Leiden: E. J. Brill, 1968), p. 8.

back in a new exodus (Isa 51:10–11) to his holy mountain (Isa 27:13).

The Judgment of Jerusalem
(*Second Temple*)

The destruction of the city and the temple of Jerusalem prophesied by Christ (Matt 24:1–2) is described as being comparable to the final destruction of the world at the end of the age, paralleling the days of Noah (Matt 25:37–39) and the days of Lot (Luke 17:28–32). The abomination causing desolation, spoken of by Daniel the prophet, that destroys the city and the sanctuary, was to come with a flood (שֶׁטֶף; LXX, κατακλυσμός, Dan 9:26–27). This abomination in the temple was to be the sign for the faithful remnant like Lot to escape to the mountains (Matt 24:15–20; Gen 19:17). The promise of a remnant of Israel again escaping wrath is that which distinguished the judgment of Jerusalem from that of Sodom (Rom 9:29; Isa 1:9).

The Judgment of Fire

The destruction of the present cosmic order is described by Peter as comparable to the destruction of the ancient order in the flood (2 Pet 3:5–7). Christ explicitly mentions the days of Noah and the days of Lot in his description of the day of the Son of Man (Matt 24:37–39; Luke 17:26–32). The wrath of the last day will be provoked by a new abomination causing desolation in the temple of God (cf. 2 Thess 2:3–4). The *parousia* of Christ brings about the fiery overthrow of the wicked (2 Thess 2:8) and the dissolution of the present heavens and earth (2 Pet 3:10–12). While the wicked will be everlastingly destroyed (Matt 24:30; 2 Thess 1:8; 2 Pet 3:7), the redeemed will find deliverance (Matt 24:31; 2 Thess 1:7; 2 Pet 3:9), coming to Mount Zion (Heb 12:22), and setting their hope on a new heavens and a new earth in which righteousness dwells (2 Pet 3:13).

The History of Israel
(*Microcosm*)

The purpose of this section of the chapter is to demonstrate the thesis that the history of Israel (microcosm) is synthetically parallel to the history of the world (macrocosm),[9] that is, that the history of Israel from his exodi to his exiles constitutes an elaborate reconstruction of the record of prediluvian history (Genesis 1-7). The method of this study will correspond to the procedure outlined in the second chapter, "The Eschatological Structure of Genesis." The consecutive structural and literary correspondences between the histories of Israel's temples and prediluvian history will be examined in turn.

The History of Israel
(First Temple)

By introducing the scriptural history of Israel with Genesis, Moses identifies Yahweh of the exodus with Elohim of creation.[10] Consequently, the exodus–eisodus history of the hexateuch is so structured as to be a redemptive reenactment of creation.[11] The redemptive creation of Israel at the sea is cast in the same narrative style of original creation as the pillar of divine presence brings light into darkness (Exod 13:21, cf. the first creative day), the waters are divided (Exod 14:21, cf. the second creative day), and the dry land emerges (Exod 14:29, cf. the third creative day). In the wilderness the superintending care of God at the creation of Israel is paralleled to the Spirit hovering over the waters of chaos (cf. רָחַף, Gen 1:2; Deut 32:11, cf. also Isa 63:11-13), bringing forth a nation like the garden of God (Num 24:5-6). The exodus culminates in the eisodus into the paradisical Canaan, a redemptive correlative to the creative sabbath (cf. Deut 12:10; Heb 4:3-10). Finally, the tabernacle, representing cosmic order, is erected (Exodus 35-40).

[9] The historiographical interdependence between Israel and the world is explicitly indicated in Moses' Song: "When the Most High divided their inheritance to the nations, when he separated the sons of Adam, he set the boundaries of the peoples according to the number of the children of Israel," (Deut 32:8). This translation rejects the fragmented Greek evidence for the reading "sons of" or "angels of God" in view of the intertestamental fascination with angelology. Agreeing with the MT are the Targum Onkelos, Aquila, Symmachus, and Theodotion. The same interdependence is implicit in the microcosmic significance of Jerusalem's temple, (cf. Ps 78:69).

[10] Cf. Isa 40:28 with 43:15; he who created (בָּרָא) the ends of the earth is the one who created (בָּרָא) Israel.

[11] This theme is elaborately developed by Meredith G. Kline in *Images of the Spirit* (Grand Rapids: Baker, 1980), pp. 12-42.

Israel: The Man

Israel, the son of God[12] redeemed from Egypt (Hos 11:1), is commissioned to reflect the nature of God in character (cf. Lev 19:2) and conduct (cf. Exod 20:8–11). He is likewise fruitful and multiplies (פָּרָה and רָבָה, Exod 1:7, cf. Gen 1:28; Neh 9:23) according to the blessing of God, filling the land (וַתִּמָּלֵא הָאָרֶץ, Exod 1:7; cf. Gen 1:28). Israel's king, like Adam, is commanded to subdue (רָדָה, Ps 110:2; cf. רָדָה, Gen 1:28) his enemies ruling the earth (cf. Pss 2:8; 72:8).

The Fall of Israel's King

The similarity of David's sin to Adam's Fall is striking.[13] David's temptation occurs in a palace terraced with gardens (cf. Gen 3:1).[14] He is tempted by a woman, taking Bathsheba and "knowing" her contrary to the command of God (Gen 2:16–17, cf. Exod 20:14). Fearing shameful exposure of his adultery, David resorts to lying and murder non-redemptively to cover his sin (2 Sam 12:12–13, cf. the fig leaves of Gen 3:7). David, deserving death (2 Sam 12:5, cf. Gen 2:17), is graciously pardoned by God.[15] Consequent to his sin is his eastward exile from the paradisical city (2 Sam 15:23, cf. Gen 3:24)[16] and the sword not turning away from his house (2 Sam 12:10, Gen 3:24). David, like Adam, becomes the father of a fratricide (2 Sam 13:23–29, cf. Gen 4:8). This setting of brother against brother in Israel foreshadows the division of the kingdom and the moral decline of God's covenant

[12] The "son of God" suggests the image of God theology, cf. Luke 3:38; Gen 5:3.

[13] The pivotal cruciality of the sin of David to the history of Israel is seen in (1) the bifed structure of 2 Samuel, i.e., the kingdom is established and strengthened in chaps. 1–10 (by anabasis), the sin of David is imputed to the nation in chap. 12 (cf. 2 Sam 24:10–14), and chaps. 13–24 recount the disastrous consequences of the sin for the kingdom (by katabasis); (2) the genealogy of Matthew is similarly stylized showing 14 generations of the establishment of the kingdom (Abraham to David) and 14 generations of its dissolution (David to the Babylonian captivity), cf. Matt 1:17; (3) that David himself realized the national consequences of his sin is evident in his penitential psalm (Ps 51:18).

[14] Cf. Neh 3:15 with 2 Kgs 21:18, 25:4. Oriental palaces were commonly associated with such gardens, cf. 2 Kgs 21:18; Esth 1:5; 7:7.

[15] Cf. Nathan's dramatic "You are the man (אִישׁ)!" The language of the prophet ironically echoes the serpent of Eden: "You shall not die!" cf. 2 Sam 12:13 with Gen 3:4.

[16] Cf. John 18:1 and the new David.

people. Likewise, the pagan marriages of Solomon (1 Kgs 11:1–13; Neh 13:26; cf. Gen 6:2) foreshadow the spiritual apostasy of the kingdom against which the Spirit, through the prophets, would strive with the people (Neh 9:30, cf. Gen 6:3).

Conflict of the Seed

The apostasy of Israel during the divided monarchy makes political Jerusalem the city of chaos, the prophets having evaluated her sin as comparable to that of Sodom and Egypt (Amos 4:10–11; Ezek 16:23). The prophets, who are continually persecuted by political Jerusalem (Matt 5:12; 23:37, cf. Jude 14–15),[17] nevertheless direct the hope of the faithful remnant to spiritual Jerusalem, the city of true worship (Psalm 48; Isa 2:2–4). But at last the land of Judah is corrupt and filled, like the antediluvian world with violence (חָמָס, Hab 1:2, 3; 2:8, 17; Gen 6:11), whereupon the prophet Habakkuk is instructed that the Chaldeans will come upon Judah like a flood.[18]

The History of Israel
(Second Temple)

The second exodus is a new creation. Isaiah's song of comfort to the captives of Judah (51:9–11) summons the arm of the Lord, which had been displayed so powerfully in the original creation and in the Egyptian exodus, to intervene once again to turn the captivity of Zion. The imagery suggests another battle with the chaos waters that prepares a way for the people of God to return dryshod (cf. similar comfort to Israel in Isa 11:15–16). The captives who would return to Zion would be given the Spirit (Hag 2:5; cf. Isa 63:11–13). They would be encouraged regarding the promise of God to make of the wilderness a garden of Eden (Isa 51:3; cf. Num 24:5–6), they would erect again the temple (representing cosmic order, cf. Ezra 8:13),[19] and God, as he had

---

[17] The scribes and Pharisees of political Jerusalem are held responsible for the blood of all the righteous from Abel (cf. Matt 23:35; Luke 11:51), by which judgment Christ places them in the line of Cain.

[18] C. F. Keil, *Commentary on the Old Testament in Ten Volumes* (Grand Rapids: Eerdmans, n.d.) vol. 10, p. 62.

[19] The two temples in the history of Israel correspond cosmologically to the two ages of world history.

after the flood, would once again accept a sacrifice of rest (נִחֹחַ, Ezek 20:41; Gen 8:21). As the original creation had been cele-brated in song (cf. Job 38:4–7) and the exodus from Egypt had been celebrated by hymn (cf. Exod 15:1–8), it was appropriate that the exiles of the second exodus, as a new creation, should return to Zion with singing (cf. Isa 51:11; Psalm 126).

Israel: The Renewed Man

The second exodus prophecy of Hosea (11:1–12) encourages the faithful remnant that God, who called his son out of Egyptian bondage, will call his son out from Assyrian captivity as well. Jeremiah's second exodus prophecy (23:3–8) contains the promise of a restoration of Israel's commission to be fruitful and multiply (פָּרָה and רָבָה, 23:3; cf. Exod 1:7; Gen 1:28), as well as a confirma-tion of the promise that David will yet subdue the earth (23:5–6; cf. Pss 2:8; 72:8; 110:2, 6; Gen 1:28).

Israel's Fall in His King

The parallels with Israel's sin in rejecting his Messiah and the record of Adam's Fall are striking. Christ was made prisoner in a garden (John 18:1–2; cf. Gen 3:1). He who "knew" no sin was made sin (1 Cor 5:21; cf. Gen 3:7), being made shamefully naked (John 19:23–24; cf. Gen 3:7).[20] Sweating blood, crowned with thorns, and hung upon a tree (Acts 10:39; cf. Gen 3:3), Christ was made a curse (Gal 3:13; cf. Gen 3:17–19), his death bringing a sword into his house (cf. Luke 2:35; 22:36; Matt 10:34).[21]

Renewed Conflict of the Seed

Physical Jerusalem once again has become the city of chaos, the apostles comparing her to Sodom (Matt 11:24) and Egypt (Matt 2:13–18; cf. Rev 11:8). Nevertheless, the hope of the faithful

[20] Through Christ's nakedness God ironically covers the sins of his people. The use of "cover" in this sense (parallel to "forgiven") in Rom 4:7 is cited from David's psalm of forgiveness (32:1). The verb כָּסָה in this psalm is used earlier of Noah's covering (Gen 9:23).

[21] Consider the great chiastic structure of biblical theology: David's sin is imputed to the nation, while the nation's sin is imputed to Christ. In Adam all die, while all in Christ are made alive!

remnant is directed to spiritual Jerusalem (Gal 4:26; John 4:21–24; Heb 12:22; Rev 21:10) while Jerusalem below persecutes Jerusalem above (Gal 4:29; 1 Thess 2:15).

THE HISTORY OF ISRAEL: THE MICROCOSM

The First Temple

EXODUS

CREATION
1. Pillar regulates day/night; waters divide, land appears, Exod 14:20–22
2. Spirit given Israel, Isa 63:11–13, cf. Deut 32:11
3. Tabernacle (cosmic order) erected, Exod 35–40
4. Israel like Eden, Num 24:5–6
5. Rest in the land, Deut 12:10; Heb 4:3–4

ISRAEL, THE NEW MAN
1. Israel, the son of God, redeemed from Eygpt, Hos 11:1
2. Israel is fruitful, multiplies, Exod 1:7; Neh 9:23
3. Israel's King to subdue the earth, Pss 2:8; 72:8; 110:2, 6

FALL OF ISRAEL'S KING
1. David sins in garden-terraced palace, cf. Neh 3:15; 2 Kgs 21:18; cf. Est 1:5
2. David "knows" Bathsheba, 2 Sam 11:4
3. David's sin shamefully exposed, 2 Sam 11:5
4. God must cover David's sin, 2 Sam 12:12–13; Ps 32:1
5. David's sin brings sword into his house, 2 Sam 12:10

CONFLICT OF SEED
1. Political Jerusalem becomes the apostate city, like Sodom and Egypt, Amos 4:10–11; Ezek 16, 23
2. Spiritual Jerusalem becomes the city of prophetic hope, the site of true worship, Ps 48; Isa 2:2–4
3. Political Jerusalem persecutes the prophets, Heb 11:32; Acts 7:52

EXILE

JUDGMENT
1. "Waters of Noah" upon the land, Isa 54:9
2. God brings the Chaldeans to destroy city and sanctuary with a flood, Isa 7–8; 17:12–13; 2 Chron 36:17–21
3. Temple (cosmic order) destroyed, 2 Chron 36:19
4. Remnant preserved, Neh 7:6ff

The Second Temple

EXODUS

CREATION RENEWED
1. New Exodus victory over chaos waters, Isa 51:9–12; 11:15–16
2. The Spirit given to Israel, Hag 2:5
3. Temple (cosmic order) erected, Ezra 3:8–13, Hag 2:9
4. Israel like garden of God, Isa 51:3
5. God receives sacrifice of rest, Ezek 20:41

ISRAEL, RENEWED MAN
1. Israel, the son of God, redeemed from Mesopotamia, Hos 11:1–11
2. Israel to be fruitful and multiply, Jer 23:3
3. Israel's King to subdue the earth, Jer 23:5–6

ISRAEL'S FALL IN HIS KING
1. Christ made prisoner in a garden, John 18:1–2
2. Christ knew no sin was made sin, 2 Cor 5:21
3. Christ made shamefully naked, John 19:23–24
4. Christ's death a covering, Rom 4:7
5. Christ hung on a tree brings curse and a sword, Acts 10:39; Gal 3:13; Matt 10:34–36

RENEWED CONFLICT OF SEED
1. Jerusalem below a chaos, like Sodom and Egypt, Gal 4:25; Matt 11:24; 2:13–18; Rev 11:8
2. Jerusalem above a city of worship, Gal 4:26; John 4:21–24; Heb 12:22; Rev 21:10
3. Jerusalem below persecutes Jerusalem above, Gal 4:29; Matt 23:37, cf. 5:12; 1 Thess 2:15

EXILE

THE NEW JUDGMENT
1. "Days of Noah" on land, Matt 24:37–39
2. God brings prince to destroy city and sanctuary with flood, Dan 9:26; Matt 24:15
3. Temple (cosmic order) destroyed Matt 24:1–2
4. Remnant preserved, Matt 24:16; Rom 9:29

A Meditation on Genesis 1-12

The History of the World that Was
Genesis 1-7

I. *The Record of the Creation (Gen 1:1-2:3)*

1.1 *In the beginning*

From everlasting to everlasting, states the scripture, God is God (Ps 90:2); and God, dwelling above time and space in all sublime perfection (cf. John 1:1-2; 17:5, 24), was pleased so to reveal himself as to evoke the everlasting praise of those he would create (Rev 4:11). God's purposes, therefore, extended from eternity into time and his counsels reached from the invisible world to the visible. The universe was fashioned a theater and man was constituted a spectator that by observation the creature might learn of the Creator and by knowledge he might render praise to his Maker.

As an observer of nature man discerns the metaphysical by the means of the physical, the transcendent by the immanent. Such is the basis and possibility of natural theology. Nevertheless, since the fall of man has profoundly affected his spiritual perspicuity, marring every aspect of his mind and heart, there remains the necessity of a proper interpretation of natural revelation, and nature must be finally interpreted by grace. Such is the basis and possibility of biblical theology (cf. Psalm 19; Rom 1:18-25). To the Christian, scripture and faith are the Urim and Thummim by which the Creator may be known through his creation. By scripture we are instructed that the worlds were framed by the Word of God (Heb 11:1), by faith we believe that testimony, and through faith, if God be pleased to grant it (cf. Eph 2:8-9), we may learn of God and please him in so learning (Heb 11:6).

God created the heavens and the earth[1]

Creation from nothing is a power proper to deity (John 1:3). It is the jewel in God's crown; it constitutes the divine claim to universal kingship. The creation trumpets God's imperial majesty for heaven is his throne and earth his footstool (Isa 66:1). Creation heralds God's royal counsel for he established the world by wisdom and stretched out the heavens by understanding (Prov 3:19). Creation presents the king with royal honor for the heavens declare his glory and the earth speaks his praise (Ps 19:1). Creation also reveals the sovereignty of his scepter for upon earth must his will be done as in heaven (Matt 6:10) and all things, in heaven and earth, must finally be summed up in his Son (Eph 1:10).

1:2   *The earth was without form, and void;*

Here is described the initial state of the earth, a waste both inhospitable and uninhabited. The divine Architect will take six days to bring order and fullness to the old creation, not because of any limit to his creative power, but to accommodate his revelation to man's finite faculties. The Creator will thus deliver the old creation from its original chaos processively, that each successive

---

[1] Though the doctrine of creation is the cornerstone of biblical revelation, to unbelief it has ever been a stone of stumbling. Scripture teaches that the world was born of the womb of God's will, fashioned from the frame of nothing (Heb 11:3). Consequently, the creation is everlastingly distinguished from its Creator and ever dependent upon him. Scripture also affirms that all men know from nature both of God's eternal power and divine person, though they suppress such natural testimony through unbelief (Rom 1:20). Those who would follow presently popular "scientific" alternatives to biblical creationism inevitably find themselves transferring these two universals from the Creator to the creation, for to accommodate their theories they ascribe a practical eternality to the creation (cf. the numberless ages presupposed by secular cosmogonies) and invest the impersonal universe with notions of purposive progress (cf. the teleology implicit in natural selectivity and 2 Pet 3:3-4). Thus the creation itself is invested with the eternal power and divine person of the Creator and the glory of the incorruptible God is changed for the image of man, birds, beasts and creeping things. Professing to be wise the secularists become vain in their reasonings and their new science merely perpetuates the ancient mysteries. The priest of nature survives in the evolutionist, the priest of mammon masquerades as the naturalist, and the priest of man has become the secular humanist. Thus has the idolatry of yesterday become the secularism of today and the dawn of the modern scientific age finds the sun rising upon nothing new.

state may be seen to be good and that in his consummating work it may be evident that all is very good. With perfect symmetry the six days will be divided into two triads; the first three days provide form, the last three days provide filling.

and darkness was on the face of the deep.

Shrouded in darkness and smothered by deep, the primitive earth is a somber picture of death. The work of the first triad of creative days will be to restrain the darkness and the deep, setting the bounds of the night and establishing the limits of the sea. In the old creation the darkness and the deep are restrained, but in the new creation, when that which is perfect is come, they will be removed altogether. In the Revelation, John writes that the new heavens and earth will have no more sea (Rev 21:1); neither will there by night for the glory of God will illumine the new creation and the Lamb will be the Light (Rev 21:23).

and the Spirit of God was hovering over the face of the waters.

The account of creation moves in a broad sweep from the restlessness of the Spirit to the sabbath rest of God. In the beginning the Spirit hovers over the womb of the old creation to bring forth the first Adam. In the fullness of time the womb of Mary, overshadowed by the Spirit, will bring forth the last Adam (Luke 1:35). All the sons of redemption, the children of the new creation, will at last be born of water and the Spirit of the womb of God's will (John 3:5).

1:3   *Then God said,*

The sacred author has presented God, the Father, by whom creation is decreed, and God, the Spirit, by whom creation is perfected. He also presents the eternal Word of God (John 1:1; Rev 19:13) by whom creation is accomplished (Col 1:16). With this anthropomorphic speech God begins to reveal himself to men in human categories, for the Word is God. This Word in his person is the revelation to men of the mind of God (cf. John 1:18). He is the audible representation of inaudible Spirit. He will become the visible expression of the invisible God. To perfect his revelation to men this Word will become flesh and dwell among us (John 1:14).

"Let there be light"; and there was light.

The earth in darkness had shadowed forth a picture of death. The light speaks of life; it is the work of the true Light to give life to men (John 1:4–5). God has thus ordained creation to speak in type of redemption for he who commanded light to shine out of darkness is the one who shines into the hearts of his people (2 Cor 4:6) bringing them from darkness to light (2 Pet 2:9) and making them a new creation (2 Cor 5:17). In this the type and the antitype correspond, that creation and redemption are totally the work of God, for who has known the mind of the Lord, or who has become his counselor? (Rom 11:34). The process in both is the same; the Spirit moves, the Word is spoken, and light shines in darkness. The conclusion in both is the same for the angels who sang together at the creation rejoice together over the sinner that finds repentance (cf. Job 38:6–7 and Luke 15:10).

1:4   *And God saw the light, that it was good; and God divided the light from the darkness.*   1:5   *God called the light Day, and the darkness He called Night, so the evening and the morning were the first day.*

The primeval light speaks in figure of the divine light, for Christ is called the Light of the World (John 8:12), the one who in perfection is the Father of Lights (Jas 1:17) and in splendor is the Sun of Righteousness (Mal 4:2). In the new heavens and earth the Lamb alone is the Light, the figure by which John will show redemption to be the light gilding eternity (Rev 21:23). From the old creation men learn to rejoice in the mysterious beauty and warmth of light so that in the new creation they might rejoice in the mysteries of redemption.

1:6–8   *Then God said, "Let there be a firmament in the midst of the waters, and let it divide the waters from the waters." Thus God made the firmament, and divided the waters which were under the firmament from the waters which were above the firmament; and it was so. And God called the firmament Heaven. So the evening and the morning were the second day.*

As the word of God's mouth was sufficient to divide the waters to make a world for man, so the blast of his nostrils could part the waters of the sea to make way for his people (Exod 15:10). Both creation and redemption display the mighty power of God, a sure comfort to a troubled heart. God, who in ancient times could say to the waters of chaos, "Be restrained!," and in latter times could say to the storms of Galilee, "Be still!," is able yet to speak peace to the turbulent heart.

1:9-10 Then God said, "Let the waters under the heavens be gathered together into one place, and let the dry land appear"; and it was so. And God called the dry land Earth, and the gathering together of the waters He called Seas. And God saw that it was good.

The deep being now distinguished from the dry land and the waters above and below filling their proper courses, God surveys his work, and again it is good. Such is the mystery of the Gospel that the Creator who in the beginning filled the seas and weighed out the waters by measure, in the incarnation became the Savior who filled a basin with water and washed the feet of the disciples (John 13:5).

1:11-13 Then God said, "Let the earth bring forth grass, the herb that yields seed, and the fruit tree that yields fruit according to its kind, whose seed is in itself, on the earth"; and it was so. And the earth brought forth grass, the herb that yields seed according to its kind, and the tree that yields fruit, whose seed is in itself according to its kind. And God saw that it was good. So the evening and the morning were the third day.

Once the dry land emerges from the waters, the divine Sower goes over the entire earth, bringing forth verdant pastures and forests. The evangelist will testify that he who sows the good seed is the Son of Man, and the field is the world (Matt 13:37-38). As in the old creation life was first brought forth from the earth on the third day, so the Firstfruits of the new creation must come forth from the earth on the third day according to the scriptures (1 Cor 15:4, 20).

*1:14-16   Then God said, "Let there be lights in the firmament of
the heavens to divide the day from the night; and let them be for
signs and seasons, and for days and years; and let them be for
lights in the firmament of the heavens to give light on the earth";
and it was so. Then God made two great lights; the greater light to
rule the day, and the lesser light to rule the night.*

The fourth day corresponds to the first, for on the first God
creates elemental light and on the fourth that light is particu-
larized into the sun and moon, which with the stars will fill the
heavens.

The sun itself is servant to the good pleasure of God. He can
still the sun in its heavenly course, as he did as a sign to the
Canaanites (Josh 20:12-13). He can turn the sun back in its
course, as he did as a sign to Hezekiah (Isa 38:7-8). He can darken
it entirely, as he did as a sign to the Egyptians (Exod 10:21-22).

He made the stars also.[2]

The hosts of heaven celebrate God's effortless power which
could bring solar systems into existence with a word and multiply
galaxies without number. Moses remarks briefly that the Almighty created the starry sky on the fourth day, that the heavenly
panoply was simply the work of the first Wednesday. What man
is sufficient to comprehend the power of God? (Isa 40:25-26).
What man in the bondage of sin need despair that God's arm is
shortened that it cannot redeem? (Isa 50:2).

*1:17-19   God set them in the firmament of the heavens to give
light on the earth, and to rule over the day and over the night, and
to divide the light from the darkness. And God saw that it was
good. So the evening and the morning were the fourth day.*

Scripture teaches that it is not the sun that governs the lives
of men, but the purposes of God. The sun is merely servant to the
will of God, running its course through the zodiac at the pleasure
of God, ruling the day by his appointment. The astrologer, like
the idolater, regards the creation rather than the Creator.

[2] Two words only in the Hebrew text chronicle the creation of numberless
galaxies! As angels are sometimes designated "morning stars," (Job 38:7) perhaps
they also were created on the fourth day.

1:20-23   *Then God said, "Let the waters abound with an abun-*
dance of living creatures, and let birds fly above the earth across
the face of the firmament of the heavens." So God created great
sea creatures and every living thing that moves, with which the
waters abounded, according to their kind. And God saw that it
was good. And God blessed them, saying, "Be fruitful and multi-
ply, and fill the waters in the seas, and let birds multiply on the
earth." So the evening and the morning were the fifth day.

The fifth day corresponds to the second, for on the second
God distinguished the sky and the sea, and on the fifth he fills
them with fowl and fish. The creator delights in his creation
(Psalm 104). He who delivers his people on eagle's wings is the
one who knows when the sparrow falls (Exod 19:4; Matt 10:29),
and he who makes Rahab to play in the sea is the one who governs
the fish of Galilee (Ps 104:26; John 21:6).

1:24-25   *Then God said, "Let the earth bring forth the living*
creature according to its kind: cattle and creeping thing and beast
of the earth, each according to its kind"; and it was so. And God
made the beast of the earth according to its kind, cattle according
to its kind, and everything that creeps on the earth according to its
kind. And God saw that it was good.

The sixth day corresponds to the third, for on the third God
caused the dry land to appear, and on the sixth he fills the earth
with animate life. The living creatures, cattle, creeping things,
and beasts display the wonderful wisdom of God in their great
variety and usefulness to man. The animals will be brought to
Adam to be named so that he might be instructed of God's
wisdom. They will afterwards be taken by Adam to be sacrificed
that he might be instructed of God's grace.

1:26   *Then God said, "Let Us make man in Our image, accord-*
ing to Our likeness;

Consider the gracious favor the divine Trinity bestows upon
man, for he puts his image upon him and makes him after his
own likeness. Caesar would coin his image of silver, Nebuchadnezzar would fashion his image of gold, but God creates his image
of clay and delights in an earthen vessel!

Let them have dominion over the fish of the sea, over the birds of the air, and over the cattle, over all the earth and over every creeping thing that creeps on the earth."

Surely there is mystery in this giving of dominion to man. To rule over the day and night God had made two great lights, unsurpassed in sidereal splendor and unchallenged among the heavenly hosts. But what is man to rule upon the earth? How his splendor is obscured by other animate creatures! His legs are not as strong as those of the horse, neither is his pace as swift as the gazelle. Can he leap like the locust, or mount up like the eagle? Has he strength to bridle Behemoth in the field, or to draw Leviathan from the sea with a hook? (cf. Job 38–41).

Even before Eden man's physical limitations give a glimmer of God's design to rule the mighty with the weak. In the eighth psalm, David discerns through the physical weakness in which man is created the purpose of God to magnify his strength in subduing the enemy through the suckling (Ps 8:2). And the shepherd boy who conquers Goliath detects the divine design to vanquish the avenger through the son of man (Ps 8:4). Thus God, who makes his image of dust the more to magnify his strength, ordains the character of the conflict between good and evil before the entrance of sin through the Fall (Gen 3:15). God, who takes pleasure in revealing himself to babes (Matt 11:25) and purposed to rest the government upon the shoulders of a child (Isa 9:6), manifests his strength in the weakness of man, thus to rebuke the enemy and the avenger (cf. 1 Cor 1:27).

The final realization of this divine design will be seen in the mission of Messiah, and the fulfillment of God's plan will be seen in the stables of Bethlehem—in the humblest quarters of the least among the thousands of Judah. From hence will come one that is to be Ruler in Israel (Mic 5:2). The one who cries in the cradle will command dominion in the midst of his enemies (Ps 110:2). He who sucks the breast will subdue the power of death (1 Cor 15:25–26). Such is divine doxology—that praise should be ordained from the mouth of babes and sucklings! (Ps 8:2).

1:27 *So God created man in His own image; in the image of God He created him; male and female He created them.*

If it was marvelous that God would make man in his image, it was more marvelous that God would be made in the image of man, that the eternal Word should become flesh and dwell among us (John 1:14), that we who were born after the image of earth might be born again in the image of heaven (1 Cor 15:47–49). For that deity should be clothed in dust, that the Ancient of Days should be born of a virgin, that the Holy One of Israel should be made in the likeness of sinful flesh is mystery more than the heart of a man could conceive or the tongue of an angel could speak!

1:28   *Then God blessed them, and God said to them, "Be fruitful and multiply; fill the earth and subdue it; have dominion over the fish of the sea, over the birds of the air, and over every living thing that moves on the earth."*

The first Adam, commanded to be fruitful and to rule over the beast, at last became the servant of the serpent who brought forth sons of death. The last Adam rules over the beast by slaying the dragon, the serpent of old (Rev 12:1–10; 20:2), and even now is filling the earth with a spiritual seed, the sons of eternity (1 Cor 15:20–22).

1:29–30   *And God said, "See, I have given you every herb that yields seed which is on the face of the earth, and every tree whose fruit yields seed; to you it shall be for food. Also, to every beast of the earth, to every bird of the air, and to everything that creeps on the earth, in which there is life, I have given every green herb for food"; and it was so.*

The primeval peace of the old creation suggested here prevails in the prophecy of the new creation. Once more will the lion eat straw like the ox, and the wolf will dwell with the lamb (Isa 11:6–9).

1:31   *Then God saw everything that He had made, and indeed it was very good. So the evening and the morning were the sixth day.*

In six days the Lord made heaven and earth, the sea, and all that is in them (Exod 20:11). Surely it is a lighter labor to make a

world than to save one. Scripture will call the heavens the work of
God's finger (Ps 8:3), but redemption will be called the labor of
his arm (Ps 77:15) and the travail of his soul (Isa 53:11). Surely it
displays the ruin of sin that God was able to establish the earth in
six days, but to perfect a saint must take a lifetime (Phil 1:6).
Nevertheless, he who created the world is ever able to create a
clean heart (Ps 51:10).

2:1   *Thus the heavens and the earth, and all the hosts of them,*
were finished.

This summary statement concludes the creation account.
God's creative work is now concluded. His providential work
will now commence (John 5:17; Col 1:16-17).

2:2   *And on the seventh day God ended His work which He had*
done, and He rested on the seventh day from all His work which
He had done.

Scripture often speaks of the work of God in creation as
prefiguring the work of God in redemption (cf. John 1:9). Hence
the deliverance of the earth from original chaos speaks in figure
of the deliverance of the elect from original sin (2 Cor 5:17). In
this sabbath rest of God in creation there is a sublime prefiguring
of Christ's work of redemption as the creative Son of God. At the
close of the sixth day of the week of Passion,[3] Christ will cry from
the cross, "It is finished," resting on the seventh day in the sleep of
death.

2:3   *Then God blessed the seventh day and sanctified it, because*
in it He rested from all His work which God had created and
made.

The Sabbath is made holy by God. It will be the duty of man,
by divine enablement, to keep it holy (Exod 20:8-11). Surely it is a

---

[3] John, the Apostle, models his Gospel as a chronicle of the new creation after
the Genesis account of the old creation. Both accounts are introduced by "in the
beginning" with light shining out of darkness. John begins his record with the
"book of seven signs," a record of daily events in the life of the Baptist and Christ
(cf. John 1:29, 35, 43; 2:1, 12, etc., and note further that it is one week from the
introduction of John the Baptist to the first miracle of Christ). The second part of
the record relates Christ's acts during the six days before the Passover (John 12:1).

pleasant duty to find sufficiency in God's supply, for the provision of this day of rest is made for man's temporal enjoyments (Mark 2:27), though it speaks as well of an eternal blessing (Heb 4:9). As the old creation was all of God, so the new creation is none of man and, in truth, to be a new creation is to cease from our own works of "righteousness," and to rest in God's work of redemption on our behalf (cf. 2 Cor 5:17). Such is the sabbath blessing of the saint who enters into Christ's rest (Heb 4:9), for truly his rest is glorious, and his yoke is easy (Isa 11:10; Matt 11:30).

II. *Adam, the First Man (Gen 2:4-25)*

2:4 *This is the genealogy of the heavens and the earth when they were created, in the day that the Lord God made the earth and the heavens.*

Genesis is a book of generations and genealogies and in every other instance of this "generations" formula (תּוֹלְדוֹת, cf. 5:1; 6:9; 10:1; 11:10; 25:19; 30:12; 37:1, etc.), there is a chronicling of the two seed and the two destinies (cf. Gen 3:15), but by way of figure in this instance the earth and heaven are seen as begotten of God, and the Creator is cast as the Father of the cosmos (cf. Moses in Ps 90:2).

2:5 *before any plant of the field was in the earth and before any herb of the field had grown. For the Lord God had not caused it to rain on the earth, and there was no man to till the ground;*

Moses describes the beautiful state of the virgin earth as she came from the hand of the Creator, clothed only in garments of green and arrayed simply in garlands of beauty. There was then no thistle or thorn to hinder the work of Adam and no fields of grain to bring sweat to his brow, for this is a description of the world that was, not yet a witness to disobedience and not yet subjected to vanity (cf. Rom 8:20).

2:6 *but a mist went up from the earth and watered the whole face of the ground;*

In that blissful state before man's disobedience, God was pleased to water the earth from subterranean springs. There was no need of rain as there was not yet the disobedience to occasion retributive drought, no need of a rainbow as there was not yet the instruction of redemptive grace.

2:7   *And the Lord God formed man of the dust*

Moses had written that man was made after the image of God (Gen 1:26) but lest his readers swell with pride, he records further that man's physical nature was fashioned of the dust of the ground. The divine Potter had made man not of the hues of heaven but of the colors of clay. The vessels on his wheel would come in earthen tones: red, black, yellow, tan, and brown. Surely it displays the perverseness of man's heart that the color of his skin, which he should wear as a mark of humility, becomes a badge of pride!

of the ground.

There is mystery in this first creation of man. By figure the earth brings forth the first man; the ground becomes the womb of Adam (cf. Job 1:21; Ps 139:16; Rom 8:21). As the first son of God (Luke 3:38) is born of the earth in the beginning, so in the last day the earth is in labor and travail to bring forth the sons of God (Rom 8:21–22). As the first man was created of the dust of the ground, so the sons of eternity will be redeemed from the dust of death.

and breathed into his nostrils the breath of life; and man became a living being.

Man becomes a living soul by divine spiration. He is thus distinguished among the animate creation, for as to origin the animals are all of earth (Gen 1:24) but man is half of heaven (Qoh 3:21). As the Father breathes physical life into the first Adam, the Son breathes spiritual life into the elect (John 20:22) that those who bore the image of the earthly might also bear the image of the heavenly (1 Cor 15:46–49). As it is written, the first Adam became a living soul. The last Adam became a life-giving spirit (1 Cor 15:45).

2:8 *The Lord God planted a garden eastward in Eden, and there He put the man whom He had formed.*

This garden of God was arrayed in oriental splendor such as to shame a Solomon: every flower a lesson in beauty, every tree a delight to the eye (Matt 6:28–29; Gen 2:9). Eden invited Adam to partake of the banquet of life, and creation's cornucopia was appointed to dress his table (cf. Cant 5:1). Beautiful orchards offered the sweetest of fruit, and Edenic vineyards presented the wine of joy. Frankincense perfumed the groves of cedar (cf. Canticles 4; Ezek 30:8), and rivers of delight gave drink to the mountains of myrrh (cf. Cant 8:14). The peaceful bliss of the garden was disturbed only by the song of the dove, its restful shades rustled only by the sport of the roe (cf. Cant 2:12, 17). To the oriental, the garden was the site of blessedness (Psalm 1) and the setting of love (cf. Cant 4:16).

2:9 *And out of the ground the Lord God made every tree grow that is pleasant to the sight and good for food. The tree of life was also in the midst of the garden, and the tree of the knowledge of good and evil.*

The Lord designed the garden of Eden to suit Adam's senses, the trees for beauty, the fruit for taste. The tree of life was set in the midst of the garden for prominence as the special gift of God, and the tree of knowledge was set for probation as the special test of man.

2:10 *Now a river went out of Eden to water the garden,*

The river Styx moistened the netherworld of death, but this fountain gave life to the lofty prominence of Eden. This great river of Eden was so plentiful in its sources that this one silver stream could not only fructify the garden of God but could amply supply the waters of the rivers of surrounding regions as well. This original Eden speaks in figure of the heavenly paradise, for the new Edenic mountain (cf. Rev 21:10) is watered by the river of the water of life. The source of these springs is the throne of God, and its streams give drink to the tree of life (cf. Rev 22:1–2; Zech 14:8–11).

2:11-12 *and from there it parted and became four riverheads.*
The name of the first is Pishon; it is the one which encompasses
the whole land of Havilah, where there is gold. And the gold of
that land is good. Bdellium and the onyx stone are there.

What a contrast Eden presents to the surrounding districts! It
is not in paradise that treasures of tribute may be found. Communion with the Creator was Eden's treasure, and this heavenly
jewel was far more precious than the onyx of Havilah. The tree of
life was the boast of Eden's garden, and the fruit of these boughs
gleamed far brighter than the gilded apples of the Hesperides or
the golden orchards of Midas (cf. Luke 12:15).

2:13-14 *The name of the second river is Gihon; it is the one*
which encompasses the whole land of Cush. The name of the
third river is Tigris; it is the one which goes toward the east of
Assyria. The fourth river is the Euphrates.

As Eden is the everlasting remembrance of delight, these
districts that surround her garden are eternal reminders of cruelty
and war, for in the course of these rivers more is suggested than
simple geography. From Eden to Cush to Assyria to Babylon is a
journey which chronicles the history of man. Once he is driven
from Eden, man's history is one of division and war. The river of
Eden, once beyond the hedges of the pleasant garden, divides into
several great rivers, which, like the Nile, will turn to blood. From
the land of Cush, watered by the Gihon, there would arise a
Nimrod, and a Babel would be erected. Nineveh would rise like a
tree planted by the rivers of the Tigris, and its boughs would be
fashioned into divine rods of anger and staffs of indignation. The
Euphrates is the river of Babylon, and the tears of God's captive
people would be the springs of this stream (cf. Ps 137:1).

2:15 *Then the Lord God took the man and put him in the*
garden of Eden to tend and keep it.

Eden's garden had been specially appointed to represent to
Adam the vitality and luxuriance of life in communion with the
Creator. Such blessedness is only by gracious appointment, its
enjoyment only by obedience to divine command. The Lord

brings Adam to the garden the better to teach him that divine blessing is not native to man but donative of God. Adam's commission is to serve the Lord God and to keep his covenant. Obedience will guide Adam to the blessing of God; disobedience will conduct him to God's judgment. In truth, Eden teaches that the favor of God is the bloom of abundance, the smile of his grace is the blossom of joy.

2:16–17 *And the Lord God commanded the man, saying, "Of every tree of the garden you may freely eat; but of the tree of the knowledge of good and evil you shall not eat, for in the day that you eat of it you shall surely die."*

These are the stipulations of God's covenant with Adam (cf. Hos 6:7), and from the very first man is instructed that there is a way of obedience leading to blessing and a way of disobedience leading to cursing. It is Adam's duty to keep covenant; it is death to violate it.

2:18 *And the Lord God said, "It is not good that man should be alone; I will make him a helper comparable to him."*

See the gracious blessing God bestows upon Adam, for the Lord takes note of his servant and designs to provide for his highest happiness by the supply of a wife of his favor. All other animate life had been created by the pair, but Adam was created alone that through his original loneliness he might learn the more to esteem his wife, and the better to bless his Creator.

2:19–20 *Out of the ground the Lord God formed every beast of the field and every bird of the air, and brought them to Adam to see what he would call them. And whatever Adam called each living creature, that was its name. So Adam gave names to all cattle, to the birds of the air, and to every beast of the field. But for Adam there was not found a helper comparable to him.*

The Lord had so constituted man that he required a wife, and God ordains in the naming of the animals a preparation of Adam for such a helper. The animals were brought in pairs to Adam to be named, and none among all their numberless variety would suffice to lessen human loneliness. The uniqueness of man was such that one must be taken of his substance and from his side, that she might lie upon his breast and find comfort under his arm. Such alone would be help meet for Adam.

2:21   *And the Lord God caused a deep sleep to fall on Adam, and he slept; and He took one of his ribs, and closed up the flesh in its place.*

In the sabbath rest there was a picture of the death of Christ as the Son of God, and in the sleep of Adam there is a figure of the death of Christ as the Son of Man. In this curious story of the Lord's provision of a wife for the first Adam, the scripture mysteriously speaks of God's provision of a bride for the last Adam, for this passage speaks ultimately of Christ and the church (Eph 5:28–32). Upon the first Adam, God brought the sleep of insensibility. Adam's side was wounded while he was yet in innocence, flesh and bone being taken for the physical creation of the first bride. Finally, Adam awakened to behold his bride in all her perfection. In the fullness of time God would bring upon the last Adam the sleep of death, whereupon his side would be wounded, blood and water issuing for the spiritual creation of the church, the blood for the bride's purchase, the water for her purification (John 19:34). Christ, as the last Adam, awakened in resurrection to behold his bride in all her perfection.

2.22   *Then the rib which the Lord God had taken from man He made into a woman, and He brought her to the man.*

Adam's precedence to Eve in creation (1 Tim 2:13) and the design of God to make the woman for man (1 Cor 11:8–9) suggest the scriptural reason for the submissiveness and reverence required of wives for their husbands. The scriptural duty of obedience, however, is not servile but regal (Mark 10:44). As the Son reveals through obedience the glory of the Father, the woman reflects through submission the glory of the man.

2:23   *And Adam said: "This is now bone of my bones, and flesh of my flesh; she shall be called Woman, because she was taken out of Man."*[4]

[4] Of the last Adam it will be stated that not a bone of him was broken (John 19:36) for his bride will not be created after the flesh but according to the Spirit.

Receiving his bride from the good hand of God, the awakened Adam sings out of mirth for a woman out of miracle. Adam had named the animals by his authority; now he names his wife according to his love, bestowing upon her a title of honor by sharing with her his own original name of eminence. A wife being now provided for the man, the Creator God sees everything that he has made and, behold, all is very good (cf. Gen 2:18; 1:31).

2:24 Therefore a man shall leave his father and mother and be joined to his wife, and they shall become one flesh.

From the beginning it is so, that God prepares the marriage bed for two and establishes the priority of a spiritual covenant (man to wife) over even the closest of natural relationships (man to parents; Matt 19:4–6). This covenant of Adam and his wife speaks in figure of the gracious covenant of Christ with the church (Eph 5:22–32) and the institution of marriage is appointed of God to be a visible token of an invisible union (cf. Isa 54:5; Rev 21:2).

It is consistent with the nature of this covenant claim that Christ will justly require for himself the singular fidelity of those bound to him, even to the forsaking of father and mother (cf. Matt 10:37). He who would do harm to the church touches the Bride of Christ, and the heavenly Bridegroom will zealously guard his betrothed (Acts 9:4; cf. Matt 25:31–46). As the first wife was constituted of the very flesh and bone of Adam, so the church partakes through the mysterious communion of the members of the last Adam, in faith being even now members of his body and in future receiving a body like unto his glorious body (Eph 5:30; Phil 3:21).

2:25 And they were both naked, the man and his wife, and were not ashamed.

It is true innocence that knows not to blush before men and need not seek cover from God (cf. Gen 3:7, 10). Truly Solomon, in all his glory, was not arrayed as one of these!

III. *The Fall of the First Adam (Gen 3:1-24)*

3:1   *Now the serpent was more cunning*

It is fitting that Satan should first appear in scripture in disguise. The old serpent, which is the devil and Satan, is a liar from the beginning, a master of masquerade, and a disciple of deceit (Rev 20:2; John 8:44). Though he is the prince of darkness, he comes arrayed as an angel of light (2 Cor 12:14). While he can come in a sop to Judas, he can come in a word from Peter (John 13:27; Matt 4:10). When he would tempt the Living Word, he comes quoting the Written Word (Matt 4:6). While he is presented in scripture as a red dragon for his carnage and a roaring lion for his cruelty, he comes as a serpent for his subtlety.

than any beast of the field which the Lord God had made.

God's creative providence establishes his sovereignty over temptation in general (cf. Luke 11:4) and this first testing in particular. God had given not only wisdom to the serpent, but beauty to the tree and pleasantness to the fruit (Gen 2:9). Satan would hide a supernatural craftiness behind the natural subtlety of the serpent.

And he said

Here we see the first evidence of Satan's craftiness. Consider the carriage of this Deceiver. Through what secret knowledge came this serpent upon the ability to speak? The faculty of speech is not natural even to the most crafty of the beasts of the field. Through this curious trick Satan suggests to Eve the possibility of attaining supernatural abilities far beyond the competence with which the creature had been originally endowed. Eve's mind is thus directed to unnatural ambition. Moreover, the infernal serpent who comes denying the doctrine of judgment seems himself to have escaped the consequences of rebellion. For what punishment attends the serpent's slandering of the Creator's kindness? Eve's mind is thus emboldened to rebellion.

We should be instructed from this that even in Eden appearances are deceptive. If Eve in innocence cannot walk by sight, how much less may those whose vision has been blinded by sin.

How much more are we to be warned from ignorance of Satan's devices and admonished to walk singularly by faith in God's Word, whatever the sight of our eyes may suggest!

to the woman,

Here is the second evidence of Satan's subtlety. Consider the strategy of the Tempter. Just as Satan would not assail God directly but his image, so he will not attack man directly but his bride. He will woo the weaker vessel in her weakest circumstance, engaging her attention outside the purview of her husband and ravishing her will apart from the counsel of her head. In so doing Satan mocks the divine order of government, designing to rule the woman by the serpent and the man by the woman. He will tempt Eve away from Adam that she might tempt Adam away from God. We should be warned from this lest, like Eve, we sacrifice the simplicity and purity of our espousal to our Husband, being beguiled by Satan's craftiness and having our minds corrupted from duty (cf. 2 Cor 11:2–3; Rom 7:4).

"Has God indeed said,

Here is yet another evidence of Satan's craftiness. Consider the subject of the Slanderer. He begins by undermining the Word of God, the foundation of all true obedience. He will call into question the kindness of the Creator, suggesting that divine jealousy forbids the fruit. The divine Word now assailed had spoken Adam into existence, fitted a world for his dominion, a paradise for his pleasure and a companion for his company. That Word had neglected no kindness of provision but had allowed no omission of duty. Once the Word is in doubt the deception is done. Like Eve, when we first presume to question the Word of God we find ourselves plucking poisoned fruit!

'You shall not eat of every tree of the garden'?"

God had appointed every tree upon the face of all the earth for food (Gen 1:29) and had permitted the free gathering of every tree of the garden but one (Gen 2:17). Satan's question is mischievously worded. To correct the misstatement is to enter into dialog with a devil, and to report the truth is to take measure of grace.

*3:2-3   And the woman said to the serpent, "We may eat the fruit
of the trees of the garden; but of the fruit of the tree which is in the
midst of the garden, God has said, "You shall not eat it, nor shall
you touch it, lest you die.'"*

Although God's proscription of the fruit of this tree for food
logically precluded the necessity of touching, this specific quali-
fication is not propositionally stated (cf. Gen 2:17). Eve's report
of this restriction reveals that her mind is magnifying the restraint
upon her. She is ready to believe the lie.

*3:4   And the serpent said to the woman, "You will not surely
die."*

Here is the climax of veracity violated. Here the liar adds
murder to his crimes. This is a lie large enough to slay all the sons
of Adam (Rom 5:12) accounted among whom will be the Son of
Man (Luke 3:23-38). Here Satan brandishes a two-edged sword
sharp enough for genocide and theocide. Here is likewise the
climax of cunning. The deceiver betrays man to death with the
kiss of friendship pretended. He proposes a toast to friendship by
offering to Eve the cup of the gods. An intoxicating elixir, to be
like God, but the venom of sin is in the serpent's vial.

*3:5   "For God knows that in the day you eat of it your eyes will be
opened, and you will be like God, knowing good and evil."*

The first Adam was given the image of God but would
become like God. Though he was God, the last Adam took the
likeness of man. The first Adam was motivated by pride; humility
was the character of the last Adam. The first Adam thought by
disobedience to escape death. The last Adam intended by obedience to suffer death (cf. Phil 2:5-8).

*3:6   So when the woman saw that the tree was good for food, that
it was pleasant to the eyes, and a tree desirable to make one wise,*

The serpent, having mesmerized the woman by the desir-
ability of the fruit, enchants her will to desire what is sinful. The
poisonous course of her depravity touches every aspect of her will,

infecting totally her power of choice. She begins to consider the evil fruit to be good for food. She delights her eyes in that which is disobedience. She covets a wisdom that is founded in folly (1 John 2:16).

she took of its fruit and ate.

The simplicity of sin belies its cosmic consequence. Consider the exceeding sinfulness of sin. All our poverty results from this transgression, and its relief will require the Son of Glory to empty himself of celestial splendor. All our misery is traceable to this rebellion, and for this disobedience the Son of Man will be known as a Man of Sorrows. All our sicknesses stem from this contagion, and their remedy will require the blood of the great Physician. Death passes upon all men because of this, and its shadow will give eclipse to the Sun of Righteousness.

She also gave to her husband with her, and he did eat.

Sin will be a cruel mistress for man. So subtle is her sorcery she will make a lover of a slave. She will strip Adam of innocence and clothe him with corruption. Exile is her dowry and harlotry her heritage. She will dress her table with the affliction of God's children for bread and the cup of their blood for drink. Death and the grave will be the double inheritance of her sons. Robbing Adam, at the beginning, of the tree of life in the paradise of God, she will erect, at last, a tree of death in the place of the skull.

3:7 *Then the eyes of both of them were opened, and they knew that they were naked*

The serpent had shrouded the nakedness of his lie in half-truths. Now the shroud is removed and they who would be like gods have their eyes opened, but it is only to behold their shame. The center of shame is their generative members, perhaps a suggestion of the guilt they had brought upon their seed; all the sons of Adam will be conceived in sin (Ps 51:5). By imputation of Adam's disobedience, all his sons will suffer death (Rom 5:12–19).

and they sewed fig leaves together and made themselves coverings.[5]

The leaves of so sweet a tree are put to so bitter an employment only after disobedience, for it is only then that the man and his wife undertake this frantic garment making. Moses had specifically noted the shameless state of the couple as they had been originally created (Gen 2:25). We may conclude, therefore, that the instinct to seek a covering comes only after their disobedience, for only then do they experience shame. Moreover, their shame is not before others (for there was no one else), nor before each other (for they were man and wife), but before God: "I heard Your voice in the garden, and I was afraid because I was naked; and I hid myself" (Gen 3:10; cf. Mark 5:15; John 21:7).

3:8 *And they heard the sound of the Lord God walking in the garden in the cool of the day,*

The sound of God's approach brings terror to the heart of fallen man and sends him scurrying into the forest to hide among the trees. The notice of time confirms the truth of the divine warning that judgment would come upon the very day of transgression (Gen 2:17) for consistent with the chronology of early Genesis, as the evening approaches a new day would begin (cf. Gen 1:5).

and Adam and his wife hid themselves from the presence of the Lord God among the trees of the garden.

---

[5] Knowledge of nakedness is the first consequence of sin, the first betrayal of guilt (Gen 3:7, 10). The first token of grace on behalf of the guilty couple will be God's dressing them in coats of skins (Gen 3:21). Manifestly much is made of nakedness in this passage, and as we should expect, there is great theological instruction in this search for "covering." The significance of this search seems to be that once man is a sinner he cannot confront the presence of God without a "cover." Consequently it is not for nothing that Israel's great Day of Atonement is called in Hebrew the "Day of Covering," and that the same Hebrew verb used to describe the covering of the nakedness of Noah by a literal garment is used metaphorically to describe the blessed man of the psalm whose sin is "covered," (cf. Gen 9:23; Ps 32:1; and also Rom 4:7–8). Man's sense of shame, then, and his instinct to cover his nakedness are left as a mark upon the consciousness of all mankind, offering silent but universal testimony to the pervasion of sin in the seed and the unfitness of man to stand in the presence of a holy God apart from a "covering."

The leaves being insufficient cover, the fallen couple attempts to hide among the trees (cf. John 1:48). Consider how the beginning and ending of history correspond. As Genesis records the first day of reckoning, the Apocalypse reveals the last day of wrath. Those who had no faith in life will exercise great faith in death—faith such as to displace mountains. The wicked sons of Adam will beg the mountains to move to give cover from divine displeasure, crying out to the rocks, "Fall on us and hide us from the face of Him who sits on the throne and from the wrath of the Lamb! For the great day of His wrath has come, and who is able to stand?" (Rev 6:16–17). But their cover in that day will be no more concealing than were Adam's aprons.

3:9   *Then the Lord God called to Adam and said to him, "Where are you?"*

The Lord's question is designed to bring conviction of sin, for Adam's hiding is the betrayal of his guilt (cf. Gen 4:9). Here is the beginning of redemptive history. Here is the Lord revealing himself in mercy, coming to Adam to seek and to save that which is lost (cf. Luke 19:10).

3:10   *So he said, "I heard Your voice in the garden, and I was afraid because I was naked; and I hid myself."*

So total was Adam's fall that the one originally created in the image of God is now conformed to the likeness of the serpent, uttering half-truths. Perjuring himself before God's bar of inquiry, Adam asserts that his hiding results from his nakedness, disguising his disobedience by claiming an effect of sin as the cause. So bold has the creature become that he would deceive the Creator, but he only deceives himself.

3:11   *And He said, "Who told you that you were naked? Have you eaten from the tree of which I commanded you that you should not eat?"*

Once again the question is designed to awaken the conscience, but it displays the totality of Adam's depravity in that it arouses only an alibi.

3:12   *Then the man said, "The woman whom You gave to be with me, she gave me of the tree, and I ate."*

Adam's confession is actually an attempt at personal exoneration. He claims as secondary cause the agency of his wife (*she gave me*), while smuggling in divine agency as the primary cause (*whom you gave*). Adam had once tried to hide his guilt with leaves, now he would disguise his disobedience with excuses. Such is the pattern for the rationalization of sin (cf. Jas 1:13–15).

3:13   *And the Lord God said to the woman, "What is this you have done?" And the woman said, "The serpent deceived me, and I ate."*

The divine interrogatory reveals the responsibility of the woman, though she spoke in truth that she was beguiled by the serpent (cf. 2 Cor 11:3; 1 Tim 2:14). Drawn away by her own lust she had conceived sin, and sin brought forth death (Jas 1:14–15). It was tragic irony that death should be the firstborn of the "mother of all living" (Gen 3:20).

3:14   *So the Lord God said to the serpent: "Because you have done this, you are cursed more than all cattle, and more than every beast of the field;*

There is no questioning of the serpent, no design for mercy to Satan. He is an Enemy who is no subject of grace (Jude 6). As the serpent was the most favored of God's creatures (Gen 3:1), so he becomes the most degraded. The judgment is measure for measure, establishing at the outset the *lex talionis* principle of punishment in the jurisprudence of scripture.

on your belly you shall go, and you shall eat dust all the days of your life.

The physical debasement of the serpent promises the defeat of the devil and the ultimate defeat of all Christ's enemies (cf. Ps 72:9; Luke 3:7; Rom 16:20).

3:15   *And I will put enmity between you and the woman, and between your seed and her Seed;*

This verse is the first evangel in scripture. It is the Gospel in Genesis. God is the sovereign subject, and he ordains the ever-lasting enmity between good and evil, between the church of Christ and the hosts of Satan (Rom 16:20; Rev 12:1–17). These are simple stories in this book of beginnings, but they contain pro-found teaching. They tell of light and darkness—good and evil; of gardens and graves—life and death. Here we are told of the sons of Satan and the sons of God, the children of darkness and the children of light. All the genealogies of Genesis will chronicle the outworking of this prophecy of the two seeds, as will all the genealogies throughout scripture. There will be constant and deadly conflict between those whose names are in the book of life and those whose genealogy is a book of death (1 John 3:7–12). The resolution of the conflict begun in Eden will be through the seed of a woman of Galilee. The Son that would vanquish the Serpent would have a maid for a mother (Gal 4:4). Woman, who had delivered man to sin, would deliver him a Savior.

he shall bruise your head,

Here the Son is promised victory over the Serpent. Through prophetic vision, the cross becomes a crown. The nails that pierced the feet would bruise the heel, but they would crush the head of sin (Gal 3:13). While the soldiers were binding Jesus for judgment, Christ was leading captivity captive (Eph 4:13). While they were scourging his back, he was healing his people (Isa 53:5). While they were crowning him with thorns, he was inaugurating his kingdom (John 18:37). While they were making spoil of his garments, he was despoiling principalities and powers (Col 2:15). Such is the wisdom of God—that the Son should vanquish the Serpent in taking the crafty by craftiness (1 Cor 3:19).

and you shall bruise His heel."

So terse the expression, so terrible the reality! This clause foresees the sufferings of Jesus of Nazareth upon the cross. That this prophecy might be fulfilled, the Son of Man would be delivered over to the power of the Serpent and made to drink of death and hell. That the church might drink the wine of remem-brance, Jesus must drink the cup of gall. Our sins were like the

sand of the sea for multitude, like the depths of the sea for
darkness, like the waters of the sea for weight. It would take an
ocean of wrath to "cover" them. Such was the measure of the cup
that could not be removed (Mark 14:36).

3:16   *To the woman He said: "I will greatly multiply your
sorrow and your conception; in pain you shall bring forth children; your desire shall be for your husband, and he shall rule over
you."*

God had commanded our first mother to be fruitful and
multiply (Gen 1:28). The entrance of sin, however, subjects the
work of the woman to vanity, for she will bear sons of death. As
every birth is a token of life, every begetting is a reminder of death.
The birth brings joy (John 16:21) but the begetting brings blood
and pain. Every child is a reminder of death. Birth may be celebrated with gold and frankincense (Isa 60:6) but there is always
the remembrance of death in the myrrh (Matt 2:11; cf. John
19:39–40).

3:17   *Then to Adam He said: "Because you have heeded the voice
of your wife, and have eaten from the tree of which I commanded
you, saying, 'You shall not eat of it'"*

God had commanded our first father to exercise dominion
and to subdue the earth (Gen 1:28). The entrance of sin, however,
subjects the work of the man to vanity, and man is himself in
death subdued of the earth. Wrought in an earthy womb (Ps
139:15) he returns to the womb of the earth (Rom 8:22). What
profit has a man from all his labor in which he toils under the
sun? (Qoh 1:3). Surely all is vanity!

*Cursed is the ground for your sake; in toil you shall eat of it all the
days of your life.*

Wearisome toil and inevitable death are the inheritance of all
the sons of Adam. The earth itself is subjected to vanity, a picture
of the fallen estate of our first parents. The earth groans like a
woman in labor, and it suffers under the bondage of corruption,
awaiting the redemptive work of the last Adam (Rom 8:19–22). It

is Christ who will see the travail of his soul and be satisfied
(Isa 53:11). It is he who through the resurrection will reveal the
sons of God (Rom 8:19). It is he who through the resurrection
will subdue the last enemy (1 Cor 15:25–26). It is thus the last
Adam who finishes the work of the first Adam (Gen 1:28; Eph
1:10). "So also it is written, The first man Adam became a living
being. The last Adam became a life-giving spirit" (1 Cor 15:45).

3:18 *Both thorns and thistles it shall bring forth for you.*

The thorns and thistles portend the adversity of nature. As
the cycle of conception reminded the woman of death by the show
of blood, so the thorns and thistles give bloody remembrance to
man of his mortality in the cycle of his calling.

3:19 *and you shall eat the herb of the field. In the sweat of your
face you shall eat bread till you return to the ground,*

As the first Adam took unto himself the sin of his bride, so the
last Adam took upon himself the sin of the church (Rom 8:2).
Adam's sin calls forth thorns from the earth, and for the church
they must be woven into a bloody crown for the Son of Man.
Adam's transgression will cover the brow of all mankind with
sweat for bread, and for the church there will be displayed great
drops of blood upon the brow of the Bread of Life. Adam's
disobedience will make a bed for all his sons in the dust of death,
and to impart life to all his sons there will be prepared a sepulcher
for the Prince of Life.

*for out of it you were taken; for dust you are, and to dust you shall
return."*[6]

What a rebuke to the rebel's pride! This Adam, who would
be like God, was lately fashioned out of dust that was made out of
nothing. Like Job, well might Adam repent in dust and ashes
(Job 42:6) for such in the hands of the divine Potter is matter
enough for a new creation (2 Cor 5:17).

---

[6] Paul's tracing of the course of sin in Rom 1:18–32 closely parallels God's
judgment in Gen 3:14–19. The Apostle considers *seriatim* the beast (3:23), the
woman (3:26) and the man (3:27).

As God's warning was sure—that disobedience would bring death—so the divine judgment is certain, and decay comes to all. Man's individual history is ever so transitory and terminal. Though his youth appear for a while fragrant and comely as the flower of the field, it is ever so fragile for he is grass (1 Pet 1:24). The grass will wither, the flower fade, so the whole of his resplendence will return to ashes (Matt 6:30). The community of man is no less transitory. Man's corporate history is one of continual debasement and ultimate decay. Like Nebuchadnezzar's dream image (Daniel 2) a nation may begin its course with the appearance of incorruptible gold, but the baser elements will succeed. The silver tarnishes, the bronze corrodes, the iron rusts, and the clay returns to dust. Haunting the entire human enterprise whispers this echo from Eden, "ashes to ashes, dust to dust!"

3:20 *And Adam called his wife's name Eve, because she was the mother of all living.*

The naming of his wife is the first evidence of Adam's faith, and the restored rebel discerns the Lord's design for mercy to men. There was demonic irony in that the one whose life was derived from man should become to him the minister of death, but there is a divine irony in the appointing of the woman to be the mother of all living.

3:21 *Also for Adam and his wife the Lord God made tunics of skin,*

It is fitting that the Lord God, who was to make the last sacrifice (Heb 9:26), should make the first; to furnish the first Adam with robes of righteousness, the last Adam would suffer nakedness and shame (Ps 22:18; Matt 27:35). This slaughter is the first sermon, and there is much Gospel in it. Here the Lord provides the skins of the innocent to "cover" the shame of the guilty. In this offering of the animals, the earth first tastes innocent blood and Adam first savors unmerited favor.

and clothed them.

Consider the character of this divine portrayal of redemption. From first to last it is the Lord who is the Alpha and Omega, the Author and Finisher of salvation. God prepares not the provision only, but the application of redemption. He makes the coats and clothes the couple. He purposes, prepares, applies, and accepts the sacrifice. There is profound teaching and immense truth in this picture of redemption. From first to last, "salvation is of the Lord," (Jonah 2:9).

3:22 *Then the Lord God said, "Behold, the man has become like one of Us, to know good and evil. And now, lest he put out his hand and take also of the tree of life, and eat, and live forever,*

This verse relates the tree of knowledge and the tree of life to man and God after the Fall. Man had tasted of the knowledge of good and evil. Now emboldened he might assail the tree of life. The Lord who intervenes is the one who would taste of evil and death on Adam's behalf. To "know" in Hebrew idiom is "to have intimate acquaintance with" (cf. Gen 4:1) and well might the Lord be said to have "knowledge" of evil for he was the Lamb foreknown for slaughter before the foundation of the world (1 Pet 1:20). The Holy One who "knew" no sin became sin for us, suffering in his body the fruit of evil. The Everlasting God who was the Tree of Life died for us, suffering in his body the fruit of death.

3:23 *therefore the Lord God sent him out of the garden of Eden*

More is lost to Adam than paradise, for to taste the fruit of disobedience was to cast away fellowship with a loving Creator and to suffer the wrath of an offended God (John 3:36). The measure of the loss magnifies the rebel's disregard of God's Word. It reveals the deceitful balance that is the sinner's scales. Just as his sons would sell the Prince of Life for the price of silver, so Adam had weighed disobedience above duty. The last Adam would teach that it profits not a man to give his soul in exchange for the world (Matt 16:26), but the first Adam had given Eden for a morsel of fruit.

to till the ground from which he was taken.

Adam was the mother of Eve, and she must serve the one from whom she was taken. Likewise, the earth was the mother of man, and he must serve the one from whom he was taken. The tilling of the ground creates in man a longing for the rest of redemption (cf. Gen 5:29) by reminding him of the rest of death (1 Cor 15:32).

3:24 *So He drove out the man;*

As the garden had represented the fertility and vitality of life, exile from the garden represents the loss of that life. Adam turns his face to his mortal future. He turns from Eden to exile, from life to death, from the garden to the grave. At the next great nexus of redemptive history the garden and the grave will converge once again. As the first Adam had made a grave of a garden, the last Adam would make a garden of a grave (Luke 24:5). The first garden saw the transgression unto death, but the last garden witnessed the resurrection unto life (John 19:41).

and He placed cherubim at the east of the garden of Eden, and a flaming sword which turned every way,

Here once again is the irony of life and death, the garden and the grave. The cherubim are elsewhere in scripture called "the living ones," (cf. Ezek 1:5-10; Rev 4:6-7), and into their hand is given the sword of flame, the emblem of the divine energy of judgment and death. The images of the cherubim were woven into the veil of the temple, and they symbolically barred access to the presence of God. The rending of the veil coincided with the sacrifice of Christ's body, throwing open once again the "way which he dedicated for us, a new and living way" to the tree of life (Matt 27:51; Heb 10:20). As the first Adam in life had lost this way, the last Adam by death regained it. Because the ancient sword was awakened against the Shepherd and sheathed in his bosom (Zech 13:7), Christ could command Peter in the garden to put away the sword (John 18:11).

to guard the way

Though the dying sinner is banished from the tree of life, there yet remains a way to return. That way is Jesus (John 14:6). He is the one who invites men to eat at the banquet of life (John 5:21). To look upon the tree of Golgatha is to be healed. To partake of the tree of Calvary is to live forever. There is no sweeter feasting than upon the bread of his body, no nobler cup than the wine of his blood. There is ample sufficiency to the bread that he provides (John 6:13). The best wine is that which he sets forth (John 2:10). To the saint who perseveres upon the path of obedience he promises to give to eat of the tree of life, which is in the paradise of God (Rev 2:7).

to the tree of life.

John, the Apostle, writes of this tree in the Apocalypse. He describes a new Eden, a paradise regained. The tree is perpetually nourished by the river of the water of life as clear as crystal, issuing from the throne of God (Rev 22:1-2). It bears twelve manner of fruit and yields twelve months in the year in perennial seasons. The leaves of the tree are for the healing of the nations rather than the covering of shame (Rev 22:2). Its boughs overspread a new heaven and earth, where there is no longer any curse (Rev 22:3).

IV. *The Conflict of the Seed (Gen 4:1-5:32)*

4:1 *Now Adam knew Eve his wife,*

Such knowledge, like the tree of the garden, will bear fruit both good and evil. It is ever so with man. From the beginning there is the seed of the woman and the seed of the serpent. God had placed a great enmity between these seed (Gen 3:15) and though brothers, like Rebekah's sons, they struggle together from the womb (Gen 25:22-23; cf. Rom 9:10-13).

It is fitting that the fruit of the first womb should prefigure the nature of this enmity and that Cain and Abel should betoken the two natures and two destinies. Cain is elder brother to all who follow in the way of the wicked (Jude 11), and Abel is the first innocent to suffer in the roster of the righteous (Heb 11:4).

and she conceived and bore Cain, and said, "I have gotten a man from the Lord."

The first woman (אִשָּׁה) had been taken from man (אִישׁ: Gen 3:22-23). Now a man (אִישׁ) is taken from woman (אִשָּׁה). Being commissioned to fruitfulness according to the image of God, Eve in her procreation corresponds in figure to the divine creation. The name Cain signifies "created" or "begotten." Eve has begotten a son, but unlike the divine creation, her "creation" is not good (Gen 4:25). Her firstborn, though a man in appearance, is a devil in truth. Eve holds a murderer in her bosom and gives suck to a serpent (1 John 3:12).

4:2   *Then she bore again, this time his brother Abel.*

The second-born son is not as highly regarded as his brother, for as Cain was given a name of blessing, Abel is named for a curse, and his name signifies "vanity" (cf. הֶבֶל in Qoh 1:2). Cain, then, has primogeniture in birth and precedence in name. But God, like Jacob's blessing of Joseph's sons, often crosses his hands of grace, giving preeminence to the one least esteemed (Gen 49:9-14; cf. 1 Cor 1:27-28). Thus from the very first we are instructed regarding the sovereign elective grace of God—the sons of God are born not of blood, nor of the will of the flesh, nor of the will of man, but of God (John 1:13).

Now Abel was a keeper of sheep, but Cain was a tiller of the ground.

Both callings were equally necessary after the Fall, for man would need the animals to provide clothing and the cultivated earth for daily bread. These occupations are the basic necessities, the most fundamental economy (cf. 1 Tim 6:8). No hint is given that the one calling is nobler than the other, for Moses will lay the basis for Cain's rejection not in his calling but in his character.

4:3-4   *And in the process of time it came to pass that Cain brought an offering of the fruit of the ground to the Lord. Abel also brought of the firstlings of his flock and of their fat.*

Here is the account of the sacrifices, and the sacrifices give an account of those who bring them. Though Cain is first in worship, Abel brings the first of what is his, offering the best portion of the best of his flock. Hereby does Abel offer a more excellent sacrifice than Cain, for his is the true faith (Heb 11:4). Abel's bloody sacrifice, like the coats of skins in the garden, makes sufficient "cover" for sin. Cain, however, would make an offering of fruit, and his bloodless sacrifice, like the leaves of the fig tree, provides no sufficient "cover."

4:5 *And the Lord respected Abel and his offering, but He did not respect Cain and his offering.*

Abel brought his heart and then his sacrifice (Heb 11:4). Cain brought his sacrifice but not his heart. The New Testament witnesses to the faith of Abel, by which he was himself accepted, and then made acceptable sacrifice (Heb 11:4). Without faith it is impossible to please God (Heb 11:6), and faithless Cain is first rejected, then his sacrifice.

4:6 *And Cain was very angry, and his countenance fell. So the Lord said to Cain, "Why are you angry? And why has your countenance fallen?*

Cain reacts not with repentance but with wrath. His deeds were as evil as his sacrifice (cf. Isa 1:10–15). As deeds betray the heart, works inevitably give evidence of faith or faithlessness (Jas 2:18). The evidence of Cain's faithless heart had been an unacceptable sacrifice. The proof of his anger is his fallen countenance.

4:7 *If you do well, will you not be accepted?*

This promise must be understood within the broader context of God's sovereign outworking of history. While the offer of acceptance is genuine, thus establishing Cain's moral responsibility, its realization is not ordained, and Cain remains bound in his sin.

And if you do not do well, sin lies at the door. And its desire is for you, but you should rule over it."

This warning includes a statement of Cain's moral responsibility. "You should rule over it" is a declaration of what he "ought" to do—his divinely revealed rule of duty. The command, however, is to his condemnation, and there is no heart of obedience granted to Cain, for he is of the evil one, and his works are wicked (1 John 3:12). Just as Pharaoh would hear the divine command, "Let my people go!," Cain hears the injunction, "You should rule over it!" But just as God ordained the disobedience of Pharaoh, "I will harden his heart, and he will not let the people go," so he has sovereignly ordained the murderous anger of Cain toward his brother, "I will put enmity between . . . your seed and her Seed" (Exod 4:21; 5:1; Gen 3:15). This question comes simply to the conclusion of Paul, the Apostle, "Therefore He has mercy on whom He wills, and whom He wills He hardens" (Rom 9:18). Behold the goodness and the severity of God! Of the same clay (Adam) has the divine Potter made one vessel unto honor (Abel) and another unto dishonor (Cain; Rom 9:21).

4:8   *Now Cain talked with Abel his brother;*

The fraternal familiarity suggested by this sentence marks Cain's crime in deepest crimson through the treachery it implies. Like the serpent in paradise, this son of Satan makes pretense of friendship while plotting murder. The conversation of Cain sets the pattern for the counsel of Ahithophel (2 Samuel 15–17) and the kiss of Judas (Mark 14:44–45; cf. Ps 41:9).

and it came to pass, when they were in the field, that Cain rose against Abel his brother and killed him.

The death of righteous Abel begins the history of enmity between the seed of the woman and the seed of the serpent (Gen 3:15), and while it is a chronicle written in letters of blood (cf. Matt 23:35) it sketches out the figure of redemption. Like Christ, Abel was well pleasing to the Lord. As he presented the firstlings of his flock, the offerer himself became the offered, the priest became himself the sacrifice, and the earth was first made to drink of righteous blood. Scorned by his brother according to the flesh (cf. John 1:11), who for envy was delivered to death (cf. Matt 27:18), he yet speaks by his blood (cf. Heb 12:24).

4:9   *Then the Lord said to Cain, "Where is Abel your brother?"*

The question is designed to display the cruelty of Cain's crime as well as the hardness of his heart. It was against his mother's son that he had lifted his hand of murder. Such is the ruin of sin upon the heart's natural affections that if Cain could kill his younger brother, Amon could violate his sister, Absalom could make rebellion against his father, and Ahithophel could conspire against his king (cf. 2 Samuel 13–15).

And he said, "I do not know. Am I my brother's keeper?"

The Lord's question to this murderer provokes a response that exposes the heart of a devil. Satan was a murderer from the beginning, and he abode not in the truth (John 8:44). In Cain does the devil have a son in his own image and likeness (1 John 3:12).

4:10 *And He said, "What have you done? The voice of your brother's blood cries out to Me from the ground.*

Here is Abel, though dead, yet speaking (Heb 11:4; Rev 6:9–11). Here does the excellence of the true Abel surpass that of the first, inasmuch as Christ's blood speaks better than that of Abel (Heb 12:24). As Abel's blood cries for vengeance, Christ's blood pleads for pardon (Luke 23:34).

4:11 *So now you are cursed from the earth, which has opened its mouth to receive your brother's blood from your hand.*

This Cain, who had been loath himself to offer a bloody sacrifice, was not unwilling to bloody the ground with the spilt life of his own brother. Now, however, the cries of innocent blood come before the Judge of all the earth (Gen 18:25). Cain comes before the bar of judgment.

4:12 *When you till the ground, it shall no longer yield its strength to you.*

Cain, the tiller of the ground, had sown his brother's blood and now reaps a curse. To Cain is given the assurance of perpetual harvests as meager as his mercy. The curse in Genesis comprehends both the offender and his seed (cf. Adam, Ham), so all the line of Cain is included within this malediction. In all the technical and cultural progress to be recorded of the sons of Cain, among the city builders, cattle raisers, craftsmen, and musicians, none is recorded as excelling in agriculture (contrast, perhaps, the Sethite Lamech, Gen 5:29).

A fugitive and a vagabond you shall be on the earth."

From first to last the scripture assigns no rest to the wicked (Isa 48:22). This wretched Cain is the father of all such as have no promise of peace. They are wayfarers with no destination, refugees with no sanctuary, foundlings with no family. Their portion is to find no peace in this world or in the world to come.

4:13   *And Cain said to the Lord, "My punishment is greater than I can bear!*

Cain reacts with remorse, not repentance. There is no sorrow over a brother slain, no contrition over a God offended. This wicked Cain would judge deficient the divine justice by challenging the suitability of the judgment to the crime.

4:14   *Surely You have driven me out this day from the face of the ground; I shall be hidden from Your face; I shall be a fugitive and a vagabond on the earth, and it will happen that anyone who finds me will kill me."*

The condemnation of Cain corresponds to the judgment of Israel. Abel's murderer, the fratricide Cain, became a fugitive. Likewise, Christ's brethren put him to death (Acts 2:36), and Israel, the regicide, learned the despair of the diaspora.

Compare the timidity of Cain with the rapaciousness of Lamech, his sixth son. The sin that with Cain was like a lion's whelp crouching at the door (Gen 4:7), with Lamech is aroused and roaring, walking about seeking whom it may devour (Gen 49:9; 1 Pet 5:8). In such a manner would the scripture measure the deluge of evil prevailing in the corrupt line of Cain.

4:15 *And the Lord said to him, "Therefore, whoever kills Cain, vengeance shall be taken on him sevenfold." And the Lord set a mark on Cain, lest anyone finding him should kill him.*

This mark is not a token of grace. It is, rather, a sign of providence. Just as God would appoint the woman another righteous seed to preserve the line of redemption, so God will appoint the preservation of the seed of the serpent to give fulfillment to the prophecy regarding the history of redemption (Gen 3:15). This preservation of the contending seed will continue until the whole redemptive counsel of God finds fulfillment (cf. especially Acts 4:27; Matt 13:24–30; Revelation 12).

4:16 *Then Cain went out from the presence of the Lord*

Adam was banished from the garden, but Cain is banished from the presence of the Lord altogether, and for this banishment there is no remedy (2 Thess 1:9).

and dwelt in the land of Nod on the east of Eden.

Cain dwelt in the land of "wandering" (נוֹד). How subtle, yet how sure is the lot of the wicked to live a life of contradiction! Like those who "live" in the land of the shadow of death (cf. Isa 9:2), Cain will "dwell" in the land of wandering. Cain's sons will be the wise of the earth but the fools of heaven (1 Cor 3:19). His family will be rich in culture but poor in profession (Luke 12:21). This godless Cain, who bore the mark of God, had outwardly found his life but had inwardly lost it (Mark 8:35).

4:17 *And Cain knew his wife, and she conceived and bore Enoch. And he built a city, and called the name of the city after the name of his son—Enoch.*

Cain goes out from the presence of God and forsakes his godly parents. He must now find fellowship in his family, building a community of his own generation apart from the faith. Cain, no less than Adam, was charged with filling the earth (Gen 1:28). Like the builders of Babel, Cain will build a city and make for himself a name, lest he be scattered over the face of the earth (Gen 11:4; cf. 4:14).

4:18   *To Enoch was born Irad; and Irad begot Mehujael, and Mehujael begot Methushael, and Methushael begot Lamach.*

The names of the Cainite line are difficult to decipher, yet it is clear that these patronyms preserve a remembrance of God (cf. the theophoric אֵל in these names). These names carry a claim of godliness. Yet the history of the Cainites suggests that they, like Cain in his sacrifice, had the form of godliness but denied the power thereof (cf. 2 Tim 3:1, 5).

4:19   *Then Lamech took for himself two wives:*

Here is the first record of this exceedingly wicked man. This seventh from Adam through Cain is likely a subject of the sermons of Enoch, the seventh from Adam through Seth. Enoch railed against the ungodly of his day, whose works of ungodliness were ungodly wrought (Jude 14, 15) and Lamech's history is preserved by Moses to demonstrate the full measure of the cup of iniquity prior to the divine judgment. Lamech is introduced as he violates the divine pattern of marriage. If God should avenge Cain sevenfold, then Lamech will avenge himself seventy-seven-fold (Gen 4:24). If God gave Adam one wife, then Lamech will take two.

4:20-22   *And Adah bore Jabal. He was the father of those who dwell in tents and have livestock. His brother's name was Jubal. He was the father of all those who play the harp and flute. And as for Zillah, she also bore Tubal-Cain, an instructor of every craftsman in bronze and iron.*

Here is the record of a family remarkable for its skill but undistinguished for its piety. In Jabal they have their tents but no tent of meeting. In Jubal they have their pipes but no psalms to sing. In Tubal-Cain[7] they have their craftsman but no tabernacle to furnish.

---

[7] The name Tubal-Cain, though aphaeresis of the *Tu* and interchange of the bilabial consonants *b/v*, reads remarkably like the Latin "Vulcan," the Roman

And the sister of Tubal-Cain was Naamah.

Naamah, whose name means "pleasantness," is perhaps to be numbered among the fair daughters of men, whom the sons of God would find appealing. She has a "pleasant" name but no piety. This terse record is otherwise the only account of her.

4:23   *Then Lamech said to his wives:*
      "Adah and Zillah, hear my voice;
      O wives of Lamech, listen to my speech!

The exordium of Lamech's song is a summons to his wives. It will assemble a polygamous audience to hear a song of disobedience. This Lamech had despised the Word of God regarding the wife (Gen 2:24; cf. Matt 19:3-8). Here he commands his wives to heed the word of Lamech.

      For I have killed a man for wounding me,
      Even a young man for hurting me.

While God would display his strength through children (Ps 8:2) Lamech would display his strength upon them, and their slaughter is his praise (cf. Matt 21:16). Cain's genealogy began with a mother's joy over the birth of a boy (Gen 4:1). It concludes with a murderer's delight at the death of a youth. Lamech is in truth a son of craftiness. He disguises his disobedience by song and mirth. He comes with melody on his lips and murder in his heart. This song is the composition of cruelty; it sings of vengeance and celebrates slaughter. Here is the contempt of God's justice, the scorn of his mercy, the dare of his wrath. Such is the flood-tide of corruption in the line of Cain, that every sentiment of every stanza is only evil continually (cf. Gen 6:5).

4:24   *If Cain shall be avenged sevenfold,*
      Then Lamech seventy-sevenfold."

Here is the mighty man of old, the man of renown (cf. Gen 6:4). Here is the one who fills the earth with violence (Gen 6:13) and

---

god of fire and craftsmanship. This workmanship in bronze and iron suggests the tremendous technical advance of this race of Cainites. Iron work would not be commonly duplicated in Syro-Palestine until ca. 900 B.C.

whose right to be heard is won by his excess of slaughter. Christ
will make the reach of Lamech's sword the measure of his mercy,
the pattern of Christian forgiveness (cf. Matt 18:21–22).[8]

4:25   *And Adam knew his wife again, and she bore a son and
named him Seth, "For God has appointed another seed for me
instead of Abel, whom Cain killed."*

This is the last we hear of our first parents, and to the end
they who would eat of the forbidden tree taste fruit both good and
evil. In her bittersweet joy at the birth of her son, Eve witnesses to
her faith that God will yet grant her the seed of redemption. The
mother who had been bereaved of both her sons in one day (cf.
Gen 27:45) had been divinely appointed yet another son through
whom God, in the fulness of time, would yet grant the Redeemer
(Luke 3:38).

4:26   *And as for Seth, to him also a son was born; and he named
him Enosh. Then men began to call on the name of the Lord.*

Through the spirit of prophecy Eve had rightly named her
son, for it was through Seth that God was pleased to revive the
godly line and to perpetuate the true religion. The race of Cain
would "call the name" of Enoch, and with this earthly city begins
the carnal community among the sons of men, (cf. Gen 6:2; 11:5).
The race of Seth would "call upon the name of the Lord," and
with this holy invocation begins the covenant community among
the sons of God. With Enoch began world history, but with
Enosh began the history of the faith, and it is through this family
that God will lay the foundations of the heavenly city (cf. Heb
11:10). Here are those who call upon the Lord in true worship,
those who are in truth the sons of God (cf. Gen 6:2).

5:1   *This is the book of the genealogy of Adam*

This unique record of Adam's generations traces the antediluvian line of Seth, from whom finally the Seed had been
promised (Luke 3:38). The unique formulation "book of the
generations" of the first Adam is adapted by Matthew in his

---

[8] Read with MT against LXX (cf. Blass, Debrunner, Funk, §248).

"book of the generations" of the last Adam, tracing the post-diluvian line of Abraham, from whom finally the Seed was born (Matt 1:1).

5:4 *After he begot Seth, the days of Adam were eight hundred years; and he begot sons and daughters.*

Adam was the father of many families out of which God had chosen the lines of Cain and Seth to develop the history of redemption. Noah likewise will father many sons, of whom God will choose the lines of Canaan and Abram to continue his redemptive program.

5:18–24 *Jared lived one hundred and sixty-two years, and begot Enoch. After he begot Methuselah, Enoch walked with God three hundred years, and begot sons and daughters. So all the days of Enoch were three hundred and sixty-five years. And Enoch walked with God; and he was not, for God took him.*

Enoch was given a name known through the line of Cain, perhaps a clue to the gradual declension of the Sethite community by spiritual and physical assimilation with the Cainite community. Nevertheless, God makes of Enoch a prophet to warn the antediluvians of catastrophic judgment (Jude 14–15). This godly prophet, who walked with God (Gen 5:24), condemned the ungodly of his world, who wrought their wickedness in an ungodly manner (Jude 15). He is placed among those saints who suffered for their confession in the record of faith in Hebrews 11, and we may be sure his unique ministry reflected the striving of God's Spirit with the antediluvian world and that his unique removal was a warning of the withdrawal of grace to those who continued to corrupt themselves.

5:28–29 *Lamech lived one hundred and eighty-two years, and begot a son. And he called his name Noah, saying, "This one will comfort us concerning our work and the toil of our hands, because of the ground which the Lord has cursed."*

The Cainite Lamech contrasts strikingly with the Sethite Lamech, for the former sang of defiance while the latter prophesies of peace. Lamech, the faithful, had other sons and daughters;

Noah had brothers and sisters, all of whom were taken away by the flood. The antediluvian apostasy had by now reduced the number of the faithful only to Noah within the house of Lamech.

V. *The Judgment of the Ancient World (Genesis 6:1-7:24).*

6:1 *Now it came to pass, when men began to multiply on the face of the earth, and daughters were born to them,*

As Satan had used Eve to tempt Adam from God, so he will use the daughters of Cain to entice the sons of Seth away from their profession (cf. Gen 4:26). Men multiply on the earth by the blessing of God, and they marry by his institution. Satan, however, would ever turn God's blessing to a curse, for he would have covenant sons marry strange women, giving occasion for the sons of Seth to be unequally yoked to the daughters of Cain and promoting the fellowship of light with darkness (cf. 2 Cor 6:14; cf. also Deut 7:3-4; Judg 14:1-4; 1 Kgs 11:1-4; Ezra 9:1-2; Job 2:9).

6:2 *that the sons of God saw the daughters of men, that they were beautiful;*[9]

How well does the Adversary proportion his temptation to the hearts of men! Satan, who would try Achan with gold and Judas with silver, tempts spiritual sons with carnal beauty. The sons of Seth betray their faith and their family by taking to wife the daughters of Cain.

and they took wives for themselves of all whom they chose.

[9] The interpretation that would make the sons of God angelic apostates (cf. Job 1:6; Jude 6) violates the context of scripture. The identification of these sons of God as professors of faith (Gen 4:26) is seen in:

a. the immediate context, wherein the genealogies of Cain and of Seth are specifically traced in detail, consistently distinguishing the Cainites as corrupt and the Sethites as faithful.

b. the fundamental context (Gen 3:15) establishes the determinative enmity between these Adamic seed, for the narratives in Genesis are rooted in the prophetic oracles.

c. the theological context, which establishes the pattern of the woman used as the agent of temptation, i.e., Eve, the daughters of Lot, the daughters of the Canaanites, the wife of Uriah, the wife of Job, and the wives of the exiles.

These are the days of Noah, and they did eat and drink, marry, and give in marriage. They were unmindful of God's wrath against sin and unheedful of his warning to sinners. As it was in the beginning, so it shall be at the end (Matt 24:37).

6:3 *And the Lord said, "My Spirit shall not strive with man forever, for he is indeed flesh;*

The longsuffering of God will suffer long but not always. Even in the ancient world did the Spirit strive against the flesh until, at last, God's grace was quenched, his wrath inflamed (cf. 2 Thess 2:3, 7).

yet his days shall be one hundred and twenty years."

This postponement of the judgment Noah was to preach surely provoked the mocking question, "Where is the promise of His coming?" (cf. 2 Pet 3:4; Jude 14). Though God's wrath is delayed in mercy, it must finally come in justice. The postponing of judgment becomes the hope of the hypocrite who would reason wrath away because it is delayed in grace.

6:4 *There were giants on the earth in those days,*

When the giants are in the land, the day of judgment is at hand. Moses takes note of these mighty men of old whom God had destroyed with the flood in order to suggest the fate of the giants of Canaan (Num 13:33), whom God would destroy with the sword. The Nephilim were in the old world until the ark of Noah came to rest upon Ararat. They would be in the new land until the ark of the covenant would come to rest upon Zion (cf. 1 Chr 6:31).

and also afterward, when the sons of God came in to the daughters of men and they bore children to them. Those were the mighty men who were of old, men of renown.

When the seed are mingled the serpent rules, for these Cainite mothers hatch a brood as viprous as Cain and as vicious

as Lamech. Renowned for wickedness, these ancients become the
subject of song and legend. Like Lamech they make praise of
cruelty, and like Cain they are the sons of the wicked one (1 John
3:12).

6:5   *Then the Lord saw that the wickedness of man was great in
the earth, and that every intent of the thoughts of his heart was
only evil continually.*

In the beginning God had created all things good (Gen 1:31).
Now, however, man has corrupted the earth, marring it with
violence and corrupting it with iniquity. Man, created in the
image of God, was now mocking his Maker, provoking his
patience with wickedness and grieving his Spirit with evil intent.
Adam's disobedience had made the earth run rivers of tears and
covered the world with oceans of blood. Now his wicked sons
would bring about an inundation of wrath.

6:6   *And the Lord was sorry that He had made man on the earth,
and He was grieved in His heart.*

Surely it is a strange occasion when God repents and not the
wicked. This evil generation had refused to repent of their sin,
and so God repents of his grace, appointing a day of terrible
judgment. The repentance of God is not the repentance of man
(1 Sam 15:29) for God is the Father of Lights, whose perfections
have no shadow of turning. When men begin to walk in disobedience they turn from the sun of God's favor to walk away in the
shadow of his wrath.

6:7   *So the Lord said, "I will destroy man whom I have created
from the face of the earth, both man and beast, creeping things
and birds of the air, for I am sorry that I have made them."*

God as the Creator-King had made the earth. In judgment he
now purposes to destroy it. In the deluge of wrath that will be

poured out upon the wicked there is not one drop of injustice, for the Righteous Judge does right, even in the world's overthrow.

6:8 *But Noah found grace in the eyes of the Lord.*

The Judge of all the earth ever distinguishes the righteous from the wicked (cf. Lot, Gen 18:23; 19:29; Rahab, Josh 6:25). His eye of grace can separate out this single grain of wheat from a world of tares (cf. Matt 13:30), for Noah must be gathered to safety before judgment can come upon the sons of the wicked one (Matt 13:37–40).

6:9–10 *This is the genealogy of Noah. Noah was a just man, perfect in his generations. Noah walked with God. And Noah begot three sons: Shem, Ham and Japheth.*

That Noah was a righteous man is tribute to God's saving mercy, and that he was perfect in his generations is tribute to God's preserving grace, for all the world had corrupted itself; Noah alone remained faithful.

6:11–12 *The earth also was corrupt before God, and the earth was filled with violence. So God looked upon the earth, and indeed it was corrupt; for all flesh had corrupted their way on the earth.*

Here is a lawless world, corrupt before God and violent toward man. See how far the wickedness of Adam has been multiplied, for as to corruption the earth is fugitive before the sons of Cain, and as to violence it quakes before the race of Lamechs.

6:13–14 *And God said to Noah, "The end of all flesh has come before Me, for the earth is filled with violence through them; and behold, I will destroy them with the earth. Make yourself an ark of gopher-wood;*

There is in scripture a common grace wherein God shows kindness to all his creatures, for he who sends the refreshing dews upon the thorn as well as the flower will send the gentle rain upon the wicked as well as the just (Matt 5:45). There is also in scripture a distinguishing grace wherein God preserves his elect from the judgment poured out upon the reprobate (cf. Exod 11:4-7), and of this grace Noah and his house are made heirs. All the world is to be destroyed, but Noah is to build an ark of deliverance.

make rooms in the ark, and cover it inside and outside with pitch.

God's deliverance of Noah at the birth of the new world corresponds to the deliverance of Moses at the birth of the new nation. Both are unmistakably of divine appointment. The Lord purposes to deliver Noah with an ark daubed with pitch. He will deliver also the one who was "drawn" from the waters in an ark daubed with pitch (Exod 2:3). As Noah would deliver his household, the new Noah would deliver his people (Ps 77:16-20). As God had destroyed the adversaries of Noah with the flood, so he would destroy the enemies of Moses with the sea (Exod 15:10).

6:15-16   *And this is how you shall make it: The length of the ark shall be three hundred cubits, its width fifty cubits, and its height thirty cubits. You shall make a window for the ark, and you shall finish it to a cubit from above; and set the door of the ark in its side. You shall make it with lower, second, and third decks.*

God's commands are ever consistent with his providence, and the ark will be fashioned to withstand the depth of the deluge and furnished to endure its duration.

6:17   *And behold, I Myself am bringing the flood of waters on the earth, to destroy from under heaven all flesh in which is the breath of life; and everything that is on the earth shall die.*

The sacred author emphasizes the divine origin of the ancient overthrow: "I, behold, I do bring the flood!" The one who poured out the mighty waters upon the wicked of the old world is the one who will pour out fire and brimstone upon the wicked of the present world (2 Pet 3:7). As it was in the days of Noah, so it shall be again (Matt 24:37-39).

6:18 *But I will establish My covenant with you; and you shall go into the ark—you, your sons, your wife, and your sons' wives with you.*

In the great apostasy of the ancient world there were only eight souls saved through the water (1 Pet 3:20). One wonders with Christ if the Son of Man will find only a few faithful to be saved through the fire when he comes at the end of the present world (cf. Luke 18:8).

6:19–20 *And of every living thing of all flesh you shall bring two of every sort into the ark, to keep them alive with you; they shall be male and female. Of the birds after their kind, of animals after their kind, and of every creeping thing of the earth after its kind, two of every kind will come to you to keep them alive.*

God will preserve the inferior creatures through man, for they are needful to his service, and they will afterwards be necessary for his sustenance.

6:21 *And you shall take for yourself of all food that is eaten, and you shall gather it to yourself; and it shall be food for you and for them."*

God's instructions for building the ark were proportioned to endure the depth of the flood, and his instruction regarding the supply of the ark is proportioned to endure its duration. That even prior to the ark's construction God appointed its dimensions demonstrates that it is God who grants repentance, for he appointed an ark which would accommodate only one household. The family of Noah would be the extent of his efficacious grace.

6:22 *Thus Noah did; according to all that God commanded him, so he did.*

The apostle places Noah in the context of those men of old who suffered for their faith (Heb 11:7) but who demonstrated their righteousness through obedience. Moses commends Noah's faithfulness in the ark's construction; it was precisely according to God's command. To the world God will reveal himself in wrath as the King of Righteousness, but to the house of Noah he will reveal himself in mercy as the Prince of Peace.

7:1   *Then the Lord said to Noah, "Come into the ark, you and all your household, because I have seen that you are righteous before Me in this generation.*

In all the world the ark is the only refuge from wrath, and the Lord in mercy commands Noah and his house to enter, for to this family there is a promise of life in the midst of a generation under sentence of death. Peter preaches the gospel from this story (1 Pet 3:18-21), for as they were safe with Noah in the ark, we may be safe with Christ in the church. Those for whom Christ is Captain will sail safely through the waters of wrath, finding everlasting rest in the new heavens and new earth.

7:2-3   *You shall take with you seven each of every clean animal, a male and his female; two each of animals that are unclean, a male and his female; also seven each of birds of the air, male and female, to keep the species alive on the face of all the earth.*

As with the division of the days, God gives six of the animals to man for breed, reserving the seventh to himself for sacrifice. The Lord will also appoint the preservation of man through the three sons of Noah with their wives, while Noah himself will present the sacrifice in the new world.

7:4   *For after seven more days I will cause it to rain on the earth forty days and forty nights, and I will destroy from the face of the earth all living things that I have made."*

God had established the old world in seven days. In seven days he will destroy it. This last sabbath will issue into the destruction of all terrestrial life, and the world will return to darkness and deep. Once again the earth will be waste and void.

7:5   *And Noah did according to all that the Lord commanded him.*

Again scripture commends the obedience of Noah. Moved with godly fear Noah had in faith prepared an ark (Heb 11:7) and the one of whom the prophecy had spoken regarding rest had been busy for over a century in the work of obedience (Gen 5:29). He would be recompensed with deliverance from wrath.

7:6   *Noah was six hundred years old when the flood of waters was on the earth.*

Noah's life becomes the new calendar, for the sun is darkened, and the moon gives no light. Seedtime and harvest, cold and heat, summer and winter, and day and night must cease, for only darkness and deep are upon the earth.

7:7   *So Noah, with his sons, his wife, and his sons' wives, went into the ark because of the waters of the flood.*

Those only find safety whom God had ordained to life. The ark had been designed to accommodate the house of Noah, for God had shut up the world to disobedience, and the preaching of Noah had been a ministry of condemnation (Heb 11:7).

7:8–9   *Of clean beasts, of beasts that are unclean, of birds, and of everything that creeps on the earth, two by two they went into the ark to Noah, male and female, as God had commanded Noah.*

With a vision of these same clean and unclean animals, God would instruct Peter, the apostle to the circumcision, regarding his acceptance of the Gentiles into the church, that those which were formerly at enmity with each other should henceforth dwell in peace and unity (Acts 10:9–16). Peter makes the ark a type of the church (1 Pet 3:20–21) for in the ark did the wolf first dwell with the lamb, and the lion did eat straw like the ox (cf. Isa 11:6–10; Rom 15:8–12).

7:10   *And it came to pass after seven days that the waters of the flood were on the earth.*

The day of grace is passed. The day of judgment is at hand. The Lord vindicates the warning of Enoch and the preaching of

Noah (Jude 14-15; 2 Pet 2:5). He executes judgment, destroying the ungodly in the waters of wickedness.

7:11 *In the six hundredth year of Noah's life, in the second month, the seventeenth day of the month, on that day all the fountains of the great deep were broken up, and the windows of heaven were opened.*

The veins of the earth are opened, the waters of the deep are ruptured, and the heavens hemorrhage the rain of death. With the solemnity of an obituary does Moses write of the death of the world that was. The entire earth passes into judgment, perishing forever in the waters of the flood.

7:12 *And the rain was on the earth forty days and forty nights.*

Forty is the number of trial and testing. God, who would consume the generation of Moses in forty years destroys the generation of Noah in forty days. Christ endures forty days and nights of testing after his baptism (cf. Matt 3:16-4:2).

7:13 *On the very same day Noah and Noah's sons, Shem, Ham, and Japheth, and Noah's wife and the three wives of his sons with them, entered the ark—*

Those with whom God had established his covenant are delivered from wrath, for provision unto life has been ordained only for God's elect. As Noah had built the ark to deliver his house rather than the world, so the carpenter's Son would provide shelter for the saved rather than the lost (Matt 20:28).

7:14 *They and every beast after its kind, all cattle after their kind, every creeping thing that creeps on the earth after its kind, and every bird after its kind, every bird of every sort.*

Moses mentions the various species of animate life using the language of creation ("after its kind," cf. Gen 1:25), for their deliverance into the new world will be a new creation.

7:15-16 *And they went into the ark to Noah, two by two, of all flesh in which is the breath of life. So those that entered, male and female of all flesh, went in as God had commanded him;*

God had displayed his wisdom in the creation of the animals. Now he reveals his providence in their preservation.

and the Lord shut him in.

God's distinguishing grace makes the entrance to the ark a seal of safety to Noah, but it is the door of death to the world. Inside the ark there is light and life and the hope of a new world. In the outer darkness there is only the wailing of the wicked and the death cry of the old world. The evil generation that had mocked God's messenger and made sport of his preaching would, like the foolish virgins of the Gospel, cry "Lord, Lord, open to us," (Matt 25:11). He who is the True Door, however, has shut them out, and who is there that can open? (John 10:7; Rev 3:7; cf. the door of Lot, Gen 19:10; of the passover, Exod 12:7; of Rahab, Josh 2:19).

7:17 Now the flood was on the earth forty days. The waters increased and lifted up the ark, and it rose high above the earth.

The very waters that smother the world will save the ark, for the flood is an instrument of judgment to the wicked but a means of deliverance to Noah. Just as the ark is said to have been baptized by the flood that destroyed the wicked (1 Pet 3:20–21) and Israel is said to have been baptized by the sea that drowned the Egyptians (1 Cor 10:2), so Christ will deliver those baptized unto him, the sign of his coming being a savor of life to the righteous and a savor of death to the disobedient.

7:18 The waters prevailed and greatly increased on the earth, and the ark moved about on the surface of the waters.

Built in obedience by Noah, the ark is guided in faithfulness by God. Though the waters are mighty to prevail over the wicked, God's mercy is mightier still. Those in the ark rest safely, awaiting the dawn of deliverance in the new world.

7:19   *And the waters prevailed exceedingly on the earth, and all the high hills under the whole heaven were covered.*

The overthrow is universal, and the world that had been born of water is buried in water (2 Pet 3:6). Chaos has returned upon the earth, and everything is once again waste and void. Darkness is again upon the face of the deep.

7:20   *The waters prevailed fifteen cubits upward, and the mountains were covered.*

The waters of Noah surmount the highest peaks by the precise draught of the ark (cf. Gen 6:15) wherein we are instructed that though the mighty waters roar, and the deluge thunders, in all the tectonic upheaval and turbulent downpour of the flood God is in precise control, for the one who sends the flood is the one who planned the ark. He who promises safety to Noah is the one who weighs the waters by measure (Job 28:25).

7:21–23   *And all flesh died that moved on the earth: birds and cattle and beasts and every creeping thing that creeps on the earth, and every man. All in whose nostrils was the breath of the spirit of life, all that was on the dry land, died. So He destroyed all living things which were on the face of the ground: both man and cattle, creeping thing and bird of the air. They were destroyed from the earth. Only Noah and those who were with him in the ark remained alive.*

The Creator-God, who had made the world in wisdom, in wrath now destroys it. The primeval chaos has prevailed over creation, and the cosmos is again formless and void. Such is the terrible overthrow of the ancient world: God delivers over the generation of Noah to everlasting chaos; the Word is forever silent to the cries of the impenitent. The Spirit finds no rest upon the waters of uncleanness.

7:24   *And the waters prevailed on the earth one hundred and fifty days.*

As the depth of the waters had testified to God's sovereignty, prevailing above the mountains by fifteen cubits, so the duration of the flood testifies to his grace, prevailing upon the earth for a hundred and fifty days. If the flood had been prolonged the supplies of the ark should have been exhausted, and faith would have perished with the wicked. For the elect's sake those days are shortened (cf. Matt 24:22).

The Historical Beginnings
of the World That Is
Genesis 8-12

I. *The Record of the New Creation (Gen 8:1-22)*

8:1 *Then God remembered Noah, and every living thing, and
all the animals that were with him in the ark. And God made a
wind to pass over the earth, and the waters subsided.*

The restraint of the waters results from the remembrance of
God of his mercy toward the ark. The Creator's wrath had
brought the waters upon the earth. Only his mercy can remove
them.

8:2-3 *The fountains of the deep and the windows of heaven
were also stopped, and the rain from heaven was restrained. And
the waters receded continually from the earth. At the end of the
hundred and fifty days the waters decreased.*

Secondary causes are superintended by God to bring about a
new creation, wind and water being obedient to the divine will
(cf. Mark 4:41). The new creation is brought about gradually,
displaying the severity of divine judgment. It is, however, brought
about continually, revealing the certainty of God's merciful
purpose.

8:4-5 *Then the ark rested in the seventh month, the seventeenth
day of the month, on the mountains of Ararat. And the waters
decreased continually until the tenth month. In the tenth month,
on the first day of the month, the tops of the mountains were seen.*

The son of Lamech (cf. Gen 5:28-29), who was to bring rest upon the earth, had built an ark which now finds rest upon the mountains. The emergence of the dry land is reminiscent of the creation account (Gen 1:9-10), and the assuaging of the waters parallels this new creation with the old creation prior to the curse (Gen 3:17).

8:6-7 *So it came to pass, at the end of forty days, that Noah opened the window of the ark which he had made. Then he sent out a raven, which kept going to and fro until the waters had dried up from the earth.*

Forty days accomplished the earth's overthrow, and perhaps Noah reckoned the necessity of yet another forty days for the reestablishment of the world. He sends forth a raven as a messenger of renewal, but the old world is passed away, and the raven returns with no sign of restoration. The dimensions of the catastrophe required not a restoration of the old world but the creation of a new.

8:8-9 *He also sent out from himself a dove, to see if the waters had abated from the face of the ground. But the dove found no resting place for the sole of her foot, and she returned into the ark to him, for the waters were on the face of the whole earth. So he put out his hand and took her, and drew her into the ark to himself.*

Now begins the account of the new creation. Just as the first creation began with the earth covered with the waters of chaos, so this new creation begins with the earth covered with the waters of wickedness. As God's Spirit had found no rest hovering upon the surface of the waters, so the dove finds no rest hovering upon the face of the deep.

8:10-12 *And he waited yet another seven days, and again he sent the dove out from the ark. Then the dove came to him in the evening, and behold, a freshly plucked olive leaf was in her mouth; and Noah knew that the waters had abated from the earth. So he waited yet another seven days and sent out the dove, which did not return again to him anymore.*

Noah's sabbatical wait in the issue of the dove reveals his faith (cf. Heb 11:7) that God alone, who created the first world in six days, can deliver the earth from such an overthrow.

8:13-14   *And it came to pass in the six hundred and first year, in the first month, the first day of the month, that the waters were dried up from the earth; and Noah removed the covering of the ark and looked, and indeed the surface of the ground was dry. And in the second month, on the twenty-seventh day of the month, the earth was dried.*

The creative order is the same here as in the original creation; as God prepared the world before bringing man upon it, once again man must wait until the world is prepared.

8:15-19   *Then God spoke to Noah, saying, "Go out of the ark, you and your wife, and your sons and your sons' wives with you. Bring out with you every living thing of all flesh that is with you: birds and cattle and every creeping thing that creeps on the earth, so that they may abound on the earth, and be fruitful and multiply on the earth." So Noah went out, and his sons and his wife and his sons' wives with him. Every beast, every creeping thing, every bird, and whatever creeps on the earth, according to their families, went out of the ark.*

The word of God once again brings life upon the earth. The animals are brought out of the ark "after their kind," just as they had been created "after their kind" in the beginning. They are once again blessed with the command to be fruitful and to multiply on the earth.

8:20   *Then Noah built an altar to the Lord,*

Consider the faith of this righteous Noah. His first desire in the new world is not to see to his own necessity or that of his house (cf. Hos 1:2-4), for before he will build shelter or provide sustenance for his family he will build an altar to the Lord, providing a sacrifice to propitiate God's wrath and to petition His favor.

and took of every clean animal and of every clean bird, and offered burnt offerings on the altar.

Noah's worship displays a love that knows no logic, for God had destroyed the great abundance of animal life with water. Now Noah will reduce their tiny number yet further with fire. God, however, who desires obedience rather than sacrifice, here desires the sacrifice because of Noah's obedience, and the new world is consecrated by an acceptable sacrifice.

8:21   *And the Lord smelled the aroma of rest.*[10]

The recreation of the world out of the waters of wickedness corresponds to the first creation of the world out of the waters of chaos. God's Spirit had hovered upon the original waters, finding rest only when the old world was established upon the seventh day. The creative work of God's Spirit now finds emblematic representation in the dove of Noah hovering upon the waters of the flood. Now that the present world is established, there is a renewed representation of divine rest in the aroma of sacrifice.

Then the Lord said in His heart, "I will never again curse the ground for man's sake, although the imagination of man's heart is evil from his youth; nor will I again destroy every living thing as I have done.

Noah's faith had found favor with God, and the prophecy of Lamech (Gen 5:29) now finds fulfillment, for Noah's obedience is the occasion of God's restraining his curse upon the ground. While Noah's obedience may bring respite from the divine curse only the obedience of the true Noah will bring its removal, for of Christ only the scripture will prophesy that his rest will be glorious (Isa 11:10) and upon Christ alone the dove will find eternal rest (Matt 3:16).

8:22   *While the earth remains, seedtime and harvest, and cold and heat, and winter and summer, and day and night shall not cease."*

This promise of perpetual seasons establishes the created order for the present heavens and earth. This natural order is to endure, by divine providence, all the days of the present heavens

---

[10] Hebrew: רֵיחַ הַנִּיחֹחַ.

and earth. Noah, who had condemned the old world (Heb 11:7), now hears God's promise regarding the present world. In faith he was ever looking to the new world where he would find everlasting rest (Heb 11:13–16; cf. also 2 Pet 3:13; Rev 22:3).

II. *Noah, the New Adam (Gen 9:1–19)*

9:1   *So God blessed Noah and his sons, and said to them: "Be fruitful and multiply, and fill the earth.*

The new world has a new Adam; as the first Adam had been father to the antediluvians, Noah will be father to the post-diluvians. Adam had been given the command to fruitfulness that he might multiply upon the earth (Gen 1:28). Now Noah is given this same command, and of his sons the whole earth will be overspread (Gen 9:19).

9:2   *And the fear of you and the dread of you shall be on every beast of the earth, on every bird of the air, on all that moved on the earth, and on all the fish of the sea. They are given into your hand.*

God had brought the animals to Adam to be named (Gen 2:19). He had brought the animals to the new Adam to be delivered. Adam had ruled the animals by love, calling every creature by name. Noah must rule by fear, taming the animals to make them serviceable to man (Jas 3:7).

9:3   *Every moving thing that lives shall be food for you. I have given you all things, even as the green herbs.*

God had appointed the herbs and fruit for the sustenance of the ancient world, but now he enlarges his table and invites man to partake of flesh as well. Every creature of God is good, and nothing is to be rejected. Everything is to be received with thanksgiving (1 Tim 4:4).

9:4   *But you shall not eat flesh with its life, that is, its blood.*

The uniqueness of man is such that though he may partake of flesh for food, he may not devour it like the animals, but must see to its preparation and purity (cf. Acts 15:28–29).

9:5-7 *Surely for your lifeblood I will demand a reckoning; from the hand of every beast I will require it, and from the hand of man. From the hand of every man's brother I will require the life of man. Whoever sheds man's blood, by man his blood shall be shed; for in the image of God He made man. And as for you, be fruitful and multiply; bring forth abundantly in the earth and multiply in it."*

At the beginning of the ancient world God had made man in his own image (Gen 1:26), and Moses made this divine image the basis of the dignity of human life (Gen 1:26–27). In the ordering of the new world, Moses makes the divine image the basis of the preservation of human life. The prohibition of murder is consistent with the command to replenish the earth, and God reserves to himself alone the right to take human life, though he ordains the sword to the state as his blood avenger. Here the fundamental relation of church and state is first constituted, and Caesar himself must avenge the willful murder of other men made in the image of God. Caesar himself bears God's image in his person. He also must render unto God what is God's, and first of all obedience in this matter of capital crime.

9:8-9 *Then God spoke to Noah and to his sons with him, saying: "And as for Me, behold, I establish My covenant with you and with your descendants after you.*

Here is the statement of God's covenant with Noah, and in grace God promises to restrain the waters of wrath, that man may multiply without fear of a flood to destroy life upon the earth.

9:10 *and with every living creature that is with you: the birds, the cattle, and every beast of the earth with you, of all that go out of the ark, every beast of the earth.*

The promise of this covenant is perpetual in that the waters of Noah should not again cover the earth, and it is pervasive in that every living creature that has breath may be called upon to praise the Lord (cf. Ps 150:6).

9:11 *Thus I establish My covenant with you: Never again shall*

*all flesh be cut off by the waters of the flood; never again shall
there be a flood to destroy the earth."*

The covenant of Noah perpetuates God's promise never-
more to cleanse the wickedness of the world with a flood, for he
reserves the present heavens and earth for a purification from the
wicked with fire (2 Pet 3:7).

9:12-13 *And God said: "This is the sign of the covenant which I
make between Me and you, and every living creature that is with
you, for perpetual generations: I set My rainbow in the cloud, and
it shall be for a sign of the covenant between Me and the earth.*

The psalmist had written that God thundered from the
heavens in his overthrow of the old world, shooting his arrows of
anger and scattering the sons of wickedness (2 Sam 22:14-16).
Now the Lord sets his bow of wrath in the heavens and promises
peace to the new world.

9:14-15 *It shall be, when I bring a cloud over the earth, that the
rainbow shall be seen in the cloud; and I will remember My
covenant which is between Me and you and every living creature
of all flesh: the waters shall never again become a flood to destroy
all flesh.*

God has many weapons in his arsenal of wrath. The old
world in corruption was cleansed with a flood. The present world
in corruption will be purified with fire (2 Pet 3:5-7). The one
who brought a cloud over the earth to destroy the old world is the
one who will come in the clouds to destroy the present one
(Matt 24:30).

9:16 *The rainbow shall be in the cloud, and I will look on it to
remember the everlasting covenant between God and every living
creature of all flesh that is on the earth." And God said to Noah,
"This is the sign of the covenant which I have established between Me and all flesh that is on the earth."*

From Ararat to Armageddon the scripture is filled with judgment to glorify the righteous wrath of God. From the earthly

rainbow of Noah's covenant to the heavenly rainbow of John's vision (Rev 4:2–3) scripture reveals the grace of God by which he glorifies his mercy. The Lord in grace makes a covenant with the new world. The bow is a weapon of war, an emblem of wrath. God will now set it in the heavens as a token of grace. The Lord who makes his bow of wrath into a seven-colored arch of beauty to ornament the heavens is the one who will finally command the nations to beat their swords into plowshares and spears into pruninghooks (Mic 4:3) for the Prince of Peace takes pleasure in mercy (Mic 7:18), and the Righteous Judge delights in grace.

9:18   *Now the sons of Noah who went out of the ark were Shem, Ham, and Japheth. And Ham was the father of Canaan.*

Moses rehearses the names of those disembarking with Noah from the ark, and he takes particular note of Canaan, the son of Ham. Much of the material in the Pentateuch is polemic, for the sons of Israel must dispossess the Canaanite, and the subsequent story of Canaan's curse is the justification of Joshua's holy war. Moses has already implicitly suggested that Canaan is ripe for judgment (cf. Gen 6:4; Num 13:33), and in the prophecy of Noah he will give explicit reason for God's wrath upon the Canaanite.

9:19   *These three were the sons of Noah, and from these the whole earth was populated.*

All the earth is descended from this one house, wherein we see the blessing of God extended to all the human family, and the command of God that men should dwell upon the face of all the earth (cf. Acts 17:26).

III. *The Fall of the New Adam (Gen 9:20–29)*

9:20   *And Noah began to be a farmer,[11] and he planted a vineyard.*

[11] That Moses intentionally relates the story of Noah's sin to Adam's fall is evident in:

a. the word play in v 20, that Noah began to be a man of the earth (cf. Adam from אֲדָמָה).

b. the parallel in v 24, Noah awoke (cf. Gen 3:7a, Adam's eyes were opened) and he knew (cf. Gen 3:6, Adam knew).

c. the structural parallel—the father's sin brings blessing and cursing upon the seed.

Like Adam, Noah had partaken much of divine grace. As the father of the ancient world sinned against his Lord and brought a curse upon his seed, so this new father will bring a new curse by his iniquity. Some have suggested that Noah here invented viniculture and sinned in ignorance being insensible to the properties of wine. Christ, however, assured the disciples that before the flood they were eating and drinking (Matt 24:38; cf. 11:19), and we may be sure that Noah both knew of wine and that his sin was deliberate.

9:21   *Then he drank of the wine*

The first Adam in eating had brought death to man, and this new Adam in drinking brings a curse upon his seed. The last Adam will make both eating and drinking the tokens of his mercy to men: the cup a remembrance of his death that men might live, the bread a memorial to his curse that men might inherit blessing.

and was drunk,

Scripture consistently records the sins of justified saints, and here is a record of this great sin of Noah. There is but one transgression recorded of this Noah who was perfect in his generations. One sin only is recorded that none may despair of justification; only one that none may presume upon grace.

9:22-23   *and became uncovered in his tent. And Ham, the father of Canaan, saw the nakedness of his father, and told his brothers outside. But Shem and Japheth took a garment, laid it on both their shoulders, and went backward and covered the nakedness of their father. Their faces were turned away, and they did not see their father's nakedness.*

Noah, in the similitude of Adam's transgression, becomes shamefully naked because of his sin (cf. Gen 3:7). Like the first Adam, this new Adam will have his nakedness clothed by another (cf. Gen 3:21). The last Adam would know the shame of nakedness in his death through which he might take to himself the shame of the sin of his people and "cover" the guilt of his church (cf. John 19:23-24).

9:24 *So Noah awoke from his wine, and knew what his younger son had done to him.*

More is suggested than that Noah awoke, for like Adam his eyes were opened, and he "knew" of his sin. The mockery of Ham exposed a heart of iniquity that could sin so callously against both his God and his father. Truly the ark had given shelter to the serpent as well as the woman.

9:25–27 *Then he said: "Cursed be Canaan; a servant of servants he shall be to his brethren." And he said: "Blessed be the Lord, the God of Shem, and may Canaan be his servant. May God enlarge Japheth, and may he dwell in the tents of Shem; and may Canaan be his servant."*

The iniquity of the father is visited upon the sons, and the record of Canaan's descendants will demonstrate how much the fathers live in their sons (cf. Gen 15:16). This statement of Noah's curse and blessing parallels precisely the first curse and blessing spoken in the garden of Eden. As the serpent was promised subjection, so the sons of wickedness will be subjected to their brethren. As Adam looked to Eve to be the mother of his Deliverer, so Japheth will dwell with Shem who will be the father of Christ (Luke 3:23–36).

9:28–29 *And Noah lived after the flood three hundred and fifty years. So all the days of Noah were nine hundred and fifty years; and he died.*

Noah had lived 600 years in the ancient world, and he survived 350 years into the present world. This great patriarch, the preacher of righteousness who found favor with God, will be raised at the last day to find everlasting life in the world to come.

IV. The Beginnings of Renewed Conflict of the Seed (Gen 10:1–11:9)

10:1 *Now this is the genealogy of the sons of Noah: Shem, Ham, and Japheth. And sons were born to them after the flood.*

The genealogies of Cain and Seth had delineated the antediluvian seed of Adam, chronicling the issue of the serpent and the woman. The record of the genealogies of Noah will portray the postdiluvian seed, the Hamite and Shemite records furthering the redemptive story.

10:8-10   *Cush begot Nimrod; he began to be a mighty one on the earth. He was a mighty hunter before the Lord; therefore it is said, "Like Nimrod the mighty hunter before the Lord." And the beginning of his kingdom was Babel.*

Nimrod is the first king in the record of the beginning of nations. His capital city, Babel, becomes representative of the seat of the anti-kingdom (Isa 47:1-15; Dan 1:1; Revelation 17-18) opposed to Zion. This rebel himself becomes representative of the anti-kingdom ruler opposed to Zion's King (Psalm 2; Mic 5:4-6). The contrast between the kings of Babel and Zion is striking. Nimrod's rule is characteristic of a hunter, his cruelty becoming proverbial as he fleeces and feasts upon his subjects. What a contrast to Babel's king is Zion's Prince! Nimrod is the mighty hunter; Christ is the good Shepherd. Nimrod will rule his people; Christ will tend his flock. Nimrod rules his subjects with might and scatters his enemies with weapons of war. Christ rules his church with gentleness, gathering the lambs into his arms and carrying the ewes in his bosom (Isa 40:11; Matt 2:6).

11:1   *Now the earth had one language and one speech.*

The unity of language (and of race, cf. v 6) precedes the division of families recorded in Genesis 10 (Gen 10:5, 20, 31) and is chronologically consequent to the sin of Noah in Genesis 11. Moses presents his material thematically. The table of nations is appended to the sin of Noah in order to relate the nations to the blessings and cursings of Noah's prophecy. The history of Babel is presented as an introduction to the family of Abram (Gen 11:10-32) in order to demonstrate the distinguishing grace of God in the election of this family of Shemites out from the nations in order to bring a blessing to the nations (Gen 12:3). As it was through the earthly Babel that the nations were divided, it will be through the heavenly Zion that they will be reunited (Isa 60:1-14; Zeph 3:9-20; Acts 2:1-11; Rev 5:9-10).

11:2 *And it came to pass, as they journeyed from the east, that they found a plain in the land of Shinar, and they dwelt there.*

These collectivists had been commanded to fill the earth, but like the Cainites they will build a great cosmopolis. The strength of this wicked generation rested in their unhindered communication, an advantage which so facilitated their communal cooperation. Their evil genius is evident in their seeking out a broad valley in which to dwell, for thus would they avoid any geographical hindrances to their concerted activity. God will use the confusion of language to divide the nations, but the wickedness of man is so severe that he will reinforce that division with deserts, mountain ranges, and oceans, the better to restrain the evil of the age.

11:3 *Then they said to one another, "Come, let us make bricks and bake them thoroughly." They had brick for stone and they had asphalt for mortar.*

This is man at the zenith of power, and this tower of brick and pitch is the acme of his accomplishment. When man would build a Babel he must use clay and slime. When God would build a Zion he will lay her foundations in sapphires and arrange her stones in fair colors (Isa 54:11–12, Rev 21:19–20). Man would build his Babel up to heaven. God will bring his Zion down from heaven (Rev 21:10). In Babel would the nations walk in the darkness of disobedience. In the heavenly Zion will the nations walk in the light of the Lord (Rev 21:24).

11:4 *And they said, "Come, let us build ourselves a city,*

This verse records the resolution of these rebels to seek fulfillment of their own and not God's purpose. God would have them replenish the earth (Gen 9:1); they will build a city. If the waters of Noah correspond to the waters of chaos and the sin of Noah corresponds to the disobedience of Adam, then the Noahic Babel builders correspond to the Cainite Enoch builders, for they too had built a city to perpetuate their name (cf. Gen 11:4; 4:16).

and a tower whose top is in the heavens;

These Babel builders, like the Cainites, pretend religious profession. They will build a new Edenic mountain. They would win heaven by their reach instead of their righteousness. They will substitute achievements in height for attainments in holiness. In so doing they lay the foundations of that religious hypocrisy known as Mystery Babylon, the mother of abominations (Rev 18:5). As the true faith will be pictured as a woman arrayed with sun and moon and crowned with twelve stars (Rev 12:1-3), so the chameleon Babylon would imposture itself as a woman, though she is dressed in scarlet and is drunk with the blood of the saints (Revelation 18). This conflict of the two women, the one delivered of a Son who is the Savior (Revelation 12) and the other delivered of harlotry and abomination (Revelation 18), reflects the hostility of the seed (Gen 3:15), for the one is in truth the church, the congregation of the righteous, and the other is the world, the assembly of the reprobate. The enmity continues until the Son, of whom the church is delivered, at last destroys this Babylon the great (Revelation 18).

let us make a name for ourselves, lest we be scattered abroad over the face of the whole earth."

How men take foolish counsel together and imagine vain things! Here the race rages against God's program; they will seek their own glory, realize their own ambition. He that sits in the heavens will deride them with the name "confusion," and scatter them abroad in his sore displeasure. The Lord's Anointed will yet reside in Zion, but Babel will be broken with a rod of iron (Psalm 2; Rev 12:5). God will give the sons of Babel a name of derision, but to Abram God will give a great name (Gen 12:2).

11:5 *But the Lord came down to see the city and the tower which the sons of men had built.*

Moses mocks the colossal self-assertion of man by exposing his infinitesimal accomplishment. This great tower, which should pierce the heavens, falls so far short of the divine prominence that the Lord must "come down to see" what man is doing.

11:6 *And the Lord said, "Indeed the people are one and they all have one language, and this is what they begin to do; now nothing that they propose to do will be withheld from them.*

The surpassing technological progress of the Cainite city had been undoubtedly promoted by the unity of language, and these Babel builders, also sharing a unity of speech, undertake the building of a great metropolis (cf. Rev 18:21–22). Like their Cainite cousins, however, these rebels who make such progress in science through their unity, will likewise greatly advance in disobedience, and the judgment of diverse tongues will be necessary to restrain their ambition.

11:7 *Come, let Us go down and there confuse their language, that they may not understand one another's speech."*

This judgment of tongues at Babel will bring about the scattering of the children of men. The gift of tongues at Zion will effect the regathering of the sons of God. In the days of Peleg the nations were divided (Gen 10:25), but upon the day of Pentecost they are reunited in Christ (Acts 2), that with one accord and with one mouth they might glorify God (Rom 15:6; cf. Zephaniah 3).

11:8 *So the Lord scattered them abroad from there over the face of all the earth,*

Moses taunts these wicked rebels, for their counsel had been to build a city to prevent their dispersion. Moses makes their very words concerning what they would avoid the statement of what came to pass (cf. Gen 11:4, 7, 9).

and they ceased building the city.

As unity had been the strength of Babel, disunity was its undoing. The judgment of tongues frustrated the raising of the rebel city.

11:9 *Therefore its name is called Babel, because there the Lord confused the language of all the earth; and from there the Lord scattered them abroad over the face of all the earth.*

The name of the wicked city signified originally the "gate of God." Moses, however, derives the Hebrew name from "confused" (בָּלַל). Such is the literary sport that Moses directs against those rebels who would make for themselves a "name" (Gen 11:4). The division of man into peoples and tribes provided a more vivid backdrop for the display of God's distinguishing grace in his elective purpose. He would now create a nation of his own (cf. Exodus 19), a people easily distinguishable from other nations due to distinctive racial features as well as cultural heritage. He would enter into common covenant with them, publishing throughout the earth and throughout the ages his peculiar relationship to them by his activity on their behalf. He would reveal ever more clearly his volitional freedom in his mercy toward Israel, his inviolate holiness in his judgment of him, his gracious faithfulness in his restitution, and his absolute and abiding sovereignty in all human history.

12:7-8   *Then the Lord appeared to Abram and said, "To your descendents I will give this land." And there he built an altar to the Lord, who had appeared to him. And he moved from there to the mountain east of Bethel, and he pitched his tent with Bethel on the west and Ai on the east; there he built an altar to the Lord and called on the name of the Lord.*

The antediluvian world had built a city, and in the resolve of the builders of Babel we see that the disobedient spirit of the sons of Cain has survived in the sons of Noah. If the spirit of Enoch survives in the Babel builders, for the parallel to be complete, where may we see the spirit of Enosh, who called upon the name of the Lord (Gen 4:26)? The context of correspondences suggests the question in order to introduce the history of Abram. As with his ancestor Enosh, of Abram it will be said as well that he called upon the name of the Lord (Gen 12:8).

Made in the USA
Middletown, DE
01 March 2017